THE MEANING OF DREAMS FOR SLEEPING MAN

THE MEANING OF DREAMS FOR SLEEPING MAN

By
Vern Hansen

J & L Publications
Trinity Center, California

By the same author:
THE LAVENDER PIG

FIRST EDITION

Copyright © 1994 Vern Hansen

Production Consultant:
Ocean Tree Services

Published by J & L Publications
Post Office Box 360
Trinity Center, CA 96091-0360

Library of Congress Cataloging-In-Publication Data:

Hansen, Vern, 1918-
    The meaning of dreams for sleeping man / by Vern Hansen. -- 1st
ed.
    ISBN: 0-9634250-2-1
    1. Dream interpretation. 2. Dreams--Religious aspects. 3. New
Age movement. I. Title.
BF1091.H36 1994
154.6'3--dc20   93-42373

DEDICATION

To my sister. . .

*And to all those of her friends and students,
who, by telling her their dreams and visions,
made the writing of this book possible.*

Vivian Heeschen
1920 - 1992

AMUSEMENT PARK

The caliopie of nature
Is prancing up and down,
And the rider of her steed
Is as foolish as a clown.

For she pumps and pushes onward
In a never ending pace.
And the ride, my friend, is endless
For the transient human race.

Life on earth is like a circle
On a painted merry-go-around.
You are riding it so firmly
With its constant up and down.

The brass ring is The Truth
That you must desire to reach.
Hold to that aspiration
And The Spirit then will teach.

You'll overcome that whirligig
With its rising and its fall,
And be a part no longer
But the essence of it all.

—Vivian Heeschen

CONTENTS

"Your life in this world is like a sleeper who dreams that he has gone to sleep. He thinks, `Now, I am asleep,' unaware that he is already in a second sleep."

- Jalal-uddin Rumi

"The Lord hath poured out upon you the spirit of deep sleep, and hath closed your eyes: the prophets and your rulers, the seers hath he covered. And the vision of all is become unto you as the words of a book that is sealed. . . . "

- Isaiah 29:10-11

OUTLINE OF THE BOOK

Forward   There is but One Dreamer and you are The Dreamer. View life from two positions. The Dreamer becomes the one in whom it awakes. An individuality emerges. You and God are One.

Introduction   Dreams are one of this century's great wastes. Dream interpreter Vivian Heeschen introduced. All dreams are God's dreams of Himself. What the Talmud says of dreams. The sense of oneself as God must be regained. Understanding one's dream life and interpreting daily life as a dream. The deepest level of dreams is the spiritual level. Pineapple-upside-down-cake. Dreams come from God according to Scripture. Jung supports the idea of One Dreamer dreaming "us." What one can do, others can do. Dream manipulation through ESP. William Dement asserts the dream world is as real as the waking world. In sleep we are "absent from the body and present with the Lord." Parallels between physical life and one's dream states lays to rest our concern with death. The Awareness of Being is the only life the personal "you" experiences. Ordinary waking state is "sleep" from a higher state of waking. Quotation from *The Kasidah*. Jung said there are two souls in every man. The intent of Zen Buddhism is to unify Man with life. Dreams are not the sole province of psychologists and psychotherapists. Three short dreams illustrate how man resists unification. Jacob's statement about his dream of a ladder that reached to Heaven. Resurrection Day joke. Joke about a piece of broken mirror glass. Leaves and labeling. Dreams are not random images made up of residual biological energy.

Chapter 1   Dreams are living Scripture. Vivian's desert dream can be found in Deuteronomy 32:10.

11

Chapter 2 Dreams are reverse parables. The command to "Interpret Your Daily Life as You Do a Dream." The four levels and the seven aspects not original with Vivian. Other thinkers have set them down. Colors as symbols of the seven aspects. A dream of a girl with a yellow dress and a red apron.

Chapter 3 Story of the householders who found a discarded lamp. Conviction makes dreams manifest. The error of taking dreams literally. Example of a woman who dreamt her uncle's leg was cut off. The man who dreamt he found a dead baby in his car trunk.

Chapter 4 God asleep as Man interprets physically, mentally, and emotionally. Awake, he interprets from a fourth level. The importance of <u>metanoia</u>. Vivian's "puddling" experience. A woman who dreamt the same dream for 15 years.

Chapter 5 Awakening is gaining a new sense of self. William Blake's, "God is the eternal dreamer." We communicate our discovery to others. A TV host boxes Vivian in. Oscar Wilde's, "Every person is born a king." Easter theme dream.

Chapter 6 Secular world has probed dreams to their limit. The interpretive faculty is in all. Ann Faraday's dream. A dream is a report from the Self to the Self about the Self. Looking at dreams through the filters of borrowed thinking. *Bible* keys to the meaning of dreams. Human soul four-quartered. Unfolding of conscious understanding takes place in seven stages.

Chapter 7 God talking about himself to Himself where keyed as your person. Car at the stop-light dream. "As in Adam, in Christ all shall be made alive." Scripture is your biography. Dream of the "Story of Everyman." William Blake's, "Eternity is in love with the productions of time." Woman's images of feeling portrayed as masculine. Opposite for men. Relatives are close relationships of mentations and emotions. Human father symbolizes the Father of Creativity. Mother symbolizes ruler of <u>persona</u>. "Snow White" example. Meaning of characters dead or dying. Man who dreamt of tiny baby and faceless woman.

12

13

Chapter 15   Dreams are totally spiritual. The intensity with which Consciousness is focused in a state determines the reality of that state. Being "awake" in a dream. World of Dreams more fluid than life. Different stories on TV but only one locale. Isaiah 55, "--all will vanish like smoke." The Dreamer suspended a superior consciousness to enter life. Bristlecone Pine. The dream would constitute your life, if you didn't wake from it. You pass into new life at death to continue till "Christ be formed in you." Vivian's, "Now I lay me down to sleep," paraphrased.

Chapter 16   We wake to a higher reality when this life dream is over. All of us are conscious but some are divinely so. Scripture says, "Awake, O Sleeper," many times. Vivian's, "Everything's the same as me." Being one with the One has to be experienced. The personal self must be surrendered for the higher Self. Our convictions often become our identities. We are houses with many rooms. Dreams are searingly truthful but benign.   Matthew 24, . "There shall not be one stone." Earthquakes. Elevators falling. Clothing shredded. Awakening can be accelerated or delayed but not prevented. "Choose ye this day whom ye will serve. . . he who finds me finds life."

Chapter 17   "Blackula." Habakkuk on good and evil. Isaiah, "I form the light and create 'darkness." Put your own character down on stage with the others. The devil is l-i-v-e-d in reverse. Job's conversation between God and Satan. See what aspect of Consciousness can function in the manner made visible to you. "Blessed are they that mourn."

Chapter 18   The Tree of Good and Evil. Watergate. Nixon dream. Present I-dentity.

Chapter 19   Dream of playing chess with the devil. Dream of man on a ship. The story of Lot.

Chapter 20   Pair opposites mentally and emotionally. We assume we are already fully conscious. White woman's dream of being married to a black man. Excerpt from Nicoll on being driven by life. Remember who you really are: The Dreamer. "Depression is a tantrum." The sin against the Holy Ghost.

14

Mickey Mouse and Walt Disney. "I am the vine, ye are the branches."

Chapter 21 Joseph and his brothers in Genesis. Neville's, *The Law and the Promise*. "There is no fiction." Robertson's, *Futility*. The Story of Joseph interpreted. Vivian and Neville.

Chapter 22 How Vivian became a dream interpreter. "Interpret your daily life as you do a dream." Dream of "Paint the coast of California with a bell." Identify as the central figure of the New Testament. The first and second comings of Christ.

Chapter 23 Girl's dream of possessing "grass." Dreams, myths, and fairy tales are blossoms on the same stem. L. Frank Baum's, *The Wizard of Oz*. "The letter killeth the spirit."

Chapter 24 "Bea! Bea! Bea!" dream. "I will make you fishers of men." Dream of "The Cheaters." How you choose is what is important.

Chapter 25 Dream of torn trousers. "Independence Day" dream.

Chapter 26 The real world is that of imagination. Fertilized egg. Woman's dream of meeting Gurdjieff's students. Insight is an indicator of the awakened man. The woman's dream interpreted. Dreams show the extremity of Self-forgetfulness, or varying stages of recovery from forgetfulness. "Like a thief in the night." *Psychological Commentaries on the Teachings of Gurdjieff and Ouspensky*. The "food of impressions."

Chapter 27 Dream of frying the *National Geographic*. Acts 6:1-4, "seven men of honest report." Dream of a stolen washing machine. 1st Corinthians 12:28, the reverse order of the seven aspects of Consciousness. Amulets and the aspects.

Chapter 28 Feeding yourself Conscious food. Identify impressions as the functions of the aspects. "Remember yourself." The Christ Child's manger is your animal form. Live in the moment, not for the moment. If you're reconciling, you won't be reacting. Remember yourself at the point of incoming

15

impressions. "The wrong man with the right tools will create a wrong result." Start from the epitome as Buddha, Christ, Krishna. "The jews took up stones to stone him." Unless you believe, "I am He." "Sin" is "to miss the mark." Consciousness is beholding Itself in the imagery by which It understands Itself.

Chapter 29 You don't become "nothing" by giving up your personal sense of identity. Nicoll, on loosening the grip of personality. Visible mechanical effects are expressions of aspects of Consciousness. Woman's dream of the Salvation Army. Dream of fourth class package labeled "Occupant." 73rd Psalm, "As a dream when one awaketh, so, O Lord, when thou awakest." Dreaming is a foreshadowing of our awakening from the three-dimensional world. Prayer is the restricted Selfhood trying to contact its source. Dreams are the source trying to make contact with the restricted Selfhood. You were the only life your dream figures had.

Chapter 30 More interest in dreams today than ever before. The Talmudic dictum about dreams. Sleep laboratories regard dreams as a form of low grade thinking. Dreams are meant to develop the soul. Kitchen colander demonstration of multiplicity within unity. "Not one shall be lost in all my holy mountain." Priests after the order of Melchizedek, the prototype of Christ. You must admit to the truth of what dreams are saying about you. Maurice Nicoll's "small `I's'." Who the "redeemed" are. God is dead only if you are. You are The Totality individualizing Itself. "If God loved us so much, why didn't he come Himself?"

Last Jung regarded all dreams as meaningful. Our dreams mark our progress or show us we are "marking time." Guidelines to interpreting daily life as if a dream. Incident of the man with the blue hair and the universal joint.

Afterthoughts Freedom Barry. Dream of a wounded Marine in a Japanese hospital. Characters in a dream cannot be convinced that they are being dreamt. We're all going to wake up. A TV show host's dream of flying to Los Angeles. More of us have the possibility of awakening than do. The "bags" we are in. The mystic does not shirk from doing his share. Maurice

16

Nicoll's "good householder." Ecclesiastes, "Everything comes alike to all." Addictive drugs are not the way to awakening. Artemidorus. God, the rewarder of them that diligently seek him. Play out the end of your string. A quote from the *I Ching*.

POSTSCRIPT:

To Dream of Knowing Is to Know of Dreaming Fiction writer Ray Bradbury's, "The Illustrated Man" taken as a symbol for the Dreamer. History as a dream panorama. A Chinese emperor dreaming of a sleeping butterfly. You are That Which Conceives of Dreaming. The potential for re-dreaming is augmented to a power beyond definition.

Addendum Resources for further probing the meaning of dream-time messages. Neville Goddard. Freedom Barry.

FORWARD

The thrust of this book can be reduced to one statement: there is but One Dreamer in time and eternity and you are The Dreamer. You know it, or you don't know it. All else is commentary. But commentary is what makes book publishers and keeps them in business, so a single statement is not enough.

That you are reading these lines between the covers of a book is convincing of at least one thing: the publisher was game enough to venture into the book's production. Not that there aren't a lot of worthless ideas presented in books. There are. But it is an asset for authors to have books as a means by which ideas can be placed in reader's hands.

Not that I necessarily will convince even one reader of this book's thesis: that there is but One Dreamer and you are He. That has to be experienced to be believed. Then why bother to write this book?

For this reason: given a sufficiently large number of readers, some of them are certain to be open-minded enough to accept as a hypothesis my thesis by saying to themselves, "If there is but One

Dreamer, and I am He, maybe I'll get the evidence of it in experience."

I'm convinced that the readers who do that will have the experience.

That makes the effort of writing this book worthwhile.

In this world of duality, the way out of it, paradoxically, is to view your life and living from two positions: one, as a person among persons with a separate identity and fate; two, as The Creator's living, as your person, in a way uniquely different from all other lives being lived.

To consider yourself, here and now, only as a person among persons is to be lost in sleep.

To go to the opposite extreme is to risk falling into the megalomania of believing your person to be God. That isn't true. You do live, as person, while here in the flesh, but it is the Divine life that makes your life possible.

When The Dreamer eventually awakens from the dream of life, "He becomes," the late Neville Goddard said, "the one in whom He awakens." In the end, you find that you are God, and always were, for there is nothing else to find. And in the finding, an individuality emerges that cannot be duplicated. With no loss of identity, you and God are One.

To believe yourself to be something that you are not, is one thing; to receive evidence of being something you haven't suspected, is quite another. Eventually, life gives you that evidence both in your nightly dream world and your daily waking world, if you can read the language.

If you cannot read the language aright? Well, as the Sufis might say: if you don't understand, things <u>are</u> just as they are. If you do understand, things are <u>just</u>, as they are.

> "That which is a stone to the ordinary man is a pearl to him who knows."   - Rumi

INTRODUCTION

Does the subject of dreams and dreaming constitute one of this century's greatest wastes? Every
night, all over the world, a harvest of dreams goes
unreaped, shooting up everywhere in profusion
where men, women, and children lie sleeping.
When a new day dawns the dream images fade with
the night, or unless they are so strong emotionally
that they are called nightmares, they are soon forgotten and like a field of ripe grain unharvested, they
wither and die.

In this book you will become acquainted with
Vivian Heeschen, a California woman, who says,
"All dreams are God's dreams of Himself, experiencing life in the flesh as you, the person who you
call by your name."[1]

She suggests you think of your dreams as a
collection of letters delivered to your door nightly.
Opened and read, they can contribute to helping you
guide your life, if you acknowledge that the most
important affair of your life is to awaken to your
divinity, your spiritual identity.

---

[1] In keeping with the timeless nature of the conversations in this book,
the present tense has been retained. Vivian Heeschen left our world
on August 23, 1992.

"A dream which is not understood is like a letter which is not opened," declares the Talmud. Just as letters addressed to us but left unopened cannot contribute to our understanding, neither can dreams that are ignored or misunderstood enlighten us.

This woman offers a nearly unexplored approach to the art of dream interpreting: each of us is God who has so thoroughly forgotten Himself to live as man that the sense of oneself, as God, must be regained consciously.

Regaining it means not only understanding one's dream life but understanding and interpreting one's daily life as if it were a dream.

The author of this book is not equipped to argue for, or against, the assertion that all psychic productions that are called dreams fit, uniformly, the concept of one dream theorist over that of another. A dream can be interpreted from whatever viewpoint the theorist chooses to take. We perceive according to how we are.

Our world is our perception of it. Through a pair of red lenses the room looks red. Through blue lenses it looks blue. Each of the blind men on the road to Hindustan who grasped the elephant interpreted differently, according to the part of it he grasped. None grasped the beast entire and that is the point of this familiar story.

The deepest level of dream interpreting is the spiritual level. Take a simple analogy: unless you cut all the way to the bottom of the pan, you won't get the best part of a pineapple-upside-down cake, because that is where the goodie lies.

"The degree of conscious Self-awareness pos-
sessed by one who attempts to interpret dreams,"
Vivian Heeschen asserts, "determines what meanings
are ascribed to them, or taken from them."

Our Scriptures say that dreams come from God.
So, if a dream to a psychotherapist shows what are
called neurotic symptoms of fragmentation, it is not
the fragmentation of the person. It is the expression
in the dreaming subject of the fragmentation that
God makes to become the life of each human being.

Wherever The Dreamer stirs and begins to
wake from sleep, a reconstructive process begins.
This, too, is revealed in dreams. As changes take
place in the depths of being, your dreams change.

To take the meaning of dreams in this sense
puts the one who does so above all the blind men of
Hindustan who grapple with the elephant at ground
level, enabling him to see it entire.

Consider again the pineapple-upside-down
cake. Who has a knife to penetrate to the spiritual
depth of dreams? Those in whom a special insight
has been enlivened.

Vivian Heeschen is not alone in saying that
there is only One Dreamer dreaming "us." The late
Carl G. Jung expressed this viewpoint in his book,
Memories, Dreams, and Reflections. Every dream is
from the Self, relating something about Itself, to
Itself.

Vivian has listened to hundreds of dreams.
Some who have taken her seriously can interpret
their dreams quite well. If what one can do can be
communicated, then what can be communicated,

others can learn to do, at least to some extent. Or it can be understood, even if the precise art of dream interpreting, and it is an art--cannot be acquired by everyone immediately.

The waking world exerts a powerful pull on us. So does the dreaming world, one that we are powerless to resist. On the tide of waking consciousness, we flow toward the sandy beach of daylit awareness. Again, just as ineluctably, we are drawn down into the depths of being, taking the flotsam of daily experiences with us where it may be incorporated into our nightly apparitions.

These apparitions are clearer in their meaning for some of us than for others, netted as we are in theories and conjectures borrowed from the past. Vivian's vision is clarified compared to many who swim in the murky wells of Freudian darkness and those who seek to manipulate the dream content of others through ESP and hypnosis, instead of probing for spiritual meaning in what their own dreams are trying to tell them. But then, to fish who've always lived in an inkwell, nothing is clearer than their own wisdom.

When in nightly sleep we retreat from the three-dimensional world and enter the world of dreams, many will say it is fascinating, but unreal. William Dement, one of the most highly regarded sleep researchers, says, however, that the reality of our dream world is as valid as that of our waking world.

Or as Vivian reflects, "What better evidence is there of the Scriptural saying that to be 'absent from the body is to be present with the Lord' than the fact of our going to sleep and dreaming?"

We go to bed hoping for a good night's sleep. We close our eyes and in a matter of minutes for most of us, we drift off to deep slumber. But not for long. Before morning comes, we are catapulted into the action of a dream, perhaps several dreams, portions of which we may carry into our waking world.

Like our waking world, our dream world is an inexhaustible portrayal of One Being enlarging its capacity for expression by understanding the interactions of living human beings with each other and their environments.

Life is an eternal rhythm of this extension and retraction, this inward and outward flowing of ours on the tides of waking and sleeping awareness, eons upon eons upon eons from an unfathomable origin to an unpredictable end.

A Scripturally based appreciation of this is necessary in order to come out of the inkwell. Our Scriptures are filled with such phrases as these, "I am the first, and I am the last." "I am the Lord, and there is none else." "I form the light and create darkness: I make peace and create evil: I the Lord do all these things." "Ye are not your own." "The creature was made subject to vanity, not willingly, but by reason of him who hath subjected the same." And finally, "For my own sake will I do it . . . I will not give my glory unto another."

Wither to, dreamer?

That this human life of yours and mine will one day end, none can deny. Of necessity, we ignore this or obscure it from our constant concern, or else, how, in morbid contemplation of death, could the world's work be done?

It is practical and prudent not to harbor dark thoughts of death and the annihilation of oneself to which such thoughts can lead. All the pleasure we have in one another--the touching, the sensing, the joy, the sharing, the communication with loved ones in our existence here together--would be lost to us, if this is our constant concern.

> Cease, Man, to mourn, to weep, to wail;
> Enjoy thy shining hour of sun;
> We dance along death's icy brink,
> But is the dance less full of fun?[2]

Life is too interested in our living to the fullest to allow us to contemplate death for long. But the most silent timepiece in the world cannot halt the passing of time. Moment by moment, the minutes are struck off, dragging us onward to some rendezvous point where life ends and we move no more among those who populate this plane.

Attitudes towards death are as varied as there are human beings to consider it; and consider it, somehow, we must, whether it be to our liking or not.

This book doesn't claim to provide comfortable ways of contemplating death. Turn to the great religions and religious literature, to the inspired writings of saints, sages, poets, and philosophers--to the comfort of compassionate human counselors--at a time of bereavement.

---

[2] THE KASIDAH OF HAJI ABDU EL-YEZDI, [Citadel Press, N.Y., 1965].

This book does attempt, however, to show how nearly one's physical life parallels the life of one's dream states, to lay to rest a concern with the fact of physical death as something final with respect to your consciousness.

It will be the last fact of your living--this having "died" according to the evidence of a lifeless physical form that no longer breathes, moves, or emotes--but That Which Is aware of having identified as you is not limited to that identification.

"How can you be sure of that?" you may ask. "Isn't the unconsciousness of sleep a 'little death' into which I enter every night when I go to bed? Haven't I lost all sense of being while in that state?"

I will answer it this way, "Didn't you enter into the state willingly when you laid down to sleep? Didn't you yearn for it?"

If your body was fatigued, and if you had no problems perplexing you, likely you welcomed sleep, and sleep welcomed you. You didn't approach your bed in fear. You knew you would likely awake refreshed, and chances are you were refreshed when you awoke.

In the deepest state of sleep you have no personal sense of being. In the unconsciousness of sleep, you are neither male nor female, healthy or sick, old or young, miserable or comfortable. You lose all sense of time and space. Should you awaken suddenly, you may be surprised that instead of having slept the night away, you have slept only a few hours or a few minutes.

But when you awake from nightly sleep, what is it within you that remembers that you laid down to sleep at a certain time, at a certain place? Your Awareness of Being, of having existence, is what remembers: the essential You that is the only life the personal "you" experiences.

Trust that sense of self: One Identity lending Its life in infinite procession and display to all that It conceives Itself to be and dreams of being. If it can be shown that your ordinary waking state is a state of "sleep" from the standpoint of a higher state of waking, do you need to fear physical death more than you fear entering into sleep each night?

> Then urge to live, thou canst not die
> Till God ordains, in life then dwell;
> No dirge to him whose ear is deaf
> To sound of tinkling Camel's bell.[3]

Carl Jung said that two souls live in every man. He treated persons who had visions of events that happened hundreds of years ago, dreams that showed parallels .to ancient Indian and Chinese temple images. "We are the carriers of the entire history of mankind," he declared. "When a man is fifty years old, only one part of his being has existed for half-a-century. The other part, which also lives in his psyche, may be millions of years old."[4]

Bernard Phillips, in his introduction to D. T. Suzuki's book, *The Essentials of Zen Buddhism*, says that it is the intent of Zen to bring Man into union

---

[3] With apologies to Haji Abdu El-Yezdi.
[4] C.G. Jung, "Everyone Has Two Souls," [Neus Wiener Journal], Nov. 9, 1932. Reprinted in William McGuire and R.F.C. Hull, C.G. *Jung Speaking*, [Princeton University Press, 1977. p. 57-58].

with life and with himself. In other words, to awaken in him the knowledge of who he really is.[5]

So, too, it is the intent of great dreams to bring this about.

Dreams are no more the exclusive province of sleep researchers, psychologists, and psychotherapists than canaries are the exclusive province of cats. But following Freud, dreams were all but usurped by medical science, and the laity resigned its interest in the subject, allowing psychoanalysts and other specialists a free and open field into dream analysis. They have made fine contributions to knowledge, but present day researchers almost invariably approach the study of dreams from the wrong perspective.

Dreams cannot fulfill a unifying function in the most profound sense until they are studied from the perspective of God asleep in the world as Man. Any other view is like looking through the wrong end of a telescope. You see no stars.

"The unawakened man sees himself as in the world, but that world seems to him to be clearly something other than his very own self. This self he takes to be only a fragment of an unknown totality, a fragment now threatened, now supported by the other fragments with which it is in contact. . . His inner life exactly mirrors the outer fragmentation."[6]

His inner life mirrors as well his acceptance of, or resistance to, the unification that is his birthright. Here are three short dreams that illustrate this:

---

[5] D.T. Suzuki, *The Essentials of Zen Buddhism*, [E.P. Dutton, N.Y., 1962. p. xiii].
[6] Ibid. p. xiii.

31

A man dreams that he crawls out of his sleeping bag and is confronted by two men with a box containing a snake. They let it out saying, "It must be exercised." The snake comes toward the sleeper and raises itself to him as a cobra would do, whereupon he says to the two men, "It must be put back in the box!"

Another man dreams he is holding a stocking containing a spider. The spider crawls up the inside of the stocking toward his hand and every time it does so, he shakes it down. Finally, when the spider is almost within reach of his hand he tosses the stocking and the spider away.

A third dream is that of a young woman who sees a large spider crawl onto her foot and sting her. Its stinger breaks off in her flesh and the spider drops away and disappears.

The snake in the first dream represents Eternal Wisdom (what Jung calls the million-year-old part of the sleeper's psyche). It has been dormant (confined in a box), and when confined it represents the instincts, the sensual man. It takes Mind and Emotion (symbolized by the two men) working together to release its power. Read John 3:14 "As Moses lifted up the serpent in the wilderness, even so must the Son of man be lifted up." When the snake approaches the sleeper he rejects it. He does not want to find out what The Eternal might do.

The second man is much like the first. The spider stands for the Creative Power of The Universe for, like a spider, It spins the world out of Itself. The man is interested in the spider, but only in a playful way. He toys with it and when it attempts to reach him, he throws it aside. He doesn't want it just yet.

But the young woman in the third dream receives what The Eternal has to give her without resisting it. The "foot" symbolizes her understanding penetrated by the spider's bite. It leaves its stinger behind as it drops away, meaning that which has been given her cannot be withdrawn! As Bernard Phillips would say, "Only he who lives from his whole Self can be called truly religious, and what characterizes the life of the enlightened soul is just that it has achieved creative wholeness. Such a life is graced with absolute freedom, for its movements are authored and authorized by the whole being and are in the deepest sense unopposed. Such a one will be conspicuously distinguishable from the individual . . . still enmeshed in duality and whose life is consequently marked by tenseness and incessant struggle as he strives in vain to subdue one-half of himself to the other half."[7]

The woman bitten by the spider will live in a new sense of herself, one of wholeness, "--the life of wholeness responding to wholeness. . . the life of absolute love, of unconditional union with all that is."[8]

Mystics and poets and seers down the ages testify that to become one with The Ever Existing One is the most joyful of human experiences. It often comes with unexpected explosive force in a dazzling, unforgettable dream. As Jacob said on dreaming of

---

[7] Ibid. p. xxv.
[8] Loc. cit.

a ladder that reached to Heaven, "Surely the Lord is in this place (meaning within himself); and I knew it not." [Genesis 29:16].

When it happens to you it will be as though it had never happened before in all eternity. It will be glorious. You may feel like the drunk who stumbled into a cemetery on a dark night and passed out in a half-dug grave. On awakening at dawn and seeing tombstones all around him he cried, "What do you know? It's Resurrection Day--and I'm the first one up!"

An ignorant peasant turned up a piece of broken mirror glass while plowing. "Why, it's a picture of my dear old departed father!" he exclaimed. He tucked it into his shirt and after supper by the fireside he couldn't resist taking it out again and again for a peek at it. His wife eyed him with suspicion, and not wanting her to know of his find, he hid it among the rafters when he went to bed. But she saw where he had put it and when he was asleep she found it and carried it to the light. "Aha!" she cried triumphantly as she peered into the glass, "so that's the ugly old hag he's been running around with!"

This tale describes how a good many of us look at dreams. A French moralist, Joseph Joubert, spoke accurately when he said, "There are some minds like either convex or concave mirrors which represent objects such as they receive them, but never receive them as they are."

Suppose that on a table there are placed a fig leaf, a magnolia blossom, and a coconut. If asked what they have in common, the answer would be, "They all come from trees." This is obvious to any one with enough experience of trees. But if you showed a leaf to someone with no knowledge of trees, he could not relate the leaf to a tree. His speculations would likely fall short of the truth about it.

Leaves can be cross-classified and sorted into bins as products of nature, vegetable proteins, combustible fuels, and other categories. What does this prove about leaves other than that they can be labeled in a variety of ways? For that matter, what can be derived from the word "label" itself?

It is made up of four letters one of which, the letter "l," is used twice. We would agree that to label anything is to assign a quality, a value, a distinction to it in order to identify it as precisely as possible. Once we have labeled a thing we can close the drawer on it using the label on the drawer to recover it, if need be.

Man is a labeling animal. "Out of the ground the Lord God formed every beast of the field, and every fowl of the air; and brought them unto Adam to see what he would call them: and whatsoever Adam called every living creature, that was the name thereof." [Genesis 2:19]. We label everything. The food we eat. The people we meet. The friends we know. The thoughts that we and they think. The clothes we wear. The occupations we pursue. A drawer labeled "labels" would have to be one of the largest drawers of all.

Getting back to our tree leaves, no matter how many ways of classifying and labeling them we can think of, examining their labels tells us nothing of what it is that produces them: the tree. Leaves come from trees, shrubs, and plants so it is the source that must be examined, if leaves are to be understood.

Therein is where many sleep and dream researchers stand. They make exhaustive studies of the mechanics of dreams, the physiological phenomena attending them, with no concern as to their meaning except for superficial statements that they are random images made of the residue of biological energy left over from the day, and are meaningless.

How well does a corpuscle of light in a beam of light understand itself to be the light? As a being of self-awareness, how aware are dream researchers of being Awareness itself? Like in the piece of mirror glass turned up by the peasant's plow, the nature of our dreams we define with our own nature. "The eyes will not see when the heart wishes them to be blind," Seneca said.

A leaf, understanding that it has no origin or existence other than the tree that produced it, would be a more enlightened leaf than one without this understanding. If both leaves were capable of dreaming, the difference in their understanding would be evident in their dreams. But enough of such fanciful verbal leaf raking. Let us go on to *THE MEANING OF DREAMS FOR SLEEPING MAN.*

THE MEANING OF

DREAMS

FOR SLEEPING MAN

Chapter 1

DREAMS ARE LIVING SCRIPTURE

Vivian Heeschen, a San Francisco Bay area California woman, is a modern dream interpreter who has an immediate intuitive understanding of the symbolism that comes to us in our dreams. Many people who have listened to her interpret their dreams agree that her gift is unique.

"Except that I do not predict futures, or find lost objects as such well-known psychics as Jeane Dixon and Peter Hurkos do," she says, "and until 1965, I was totally unaware that I had this gift."

"I had no interest in dreams. I had never studied them nor any systems related to dream interpretation. I was a person who seldom dreamt, certainly with no recall. I was quite content to be an ordinary housewife and homemaker, and a rather successful independent business woman dealing in fashion hairpieces with a large sales staff and my own stylists to help me. I was one of the pioneers in that industry which now has grown tremendously, but it's a part of my life no longer.

"Now," she says laughingly, "I am not concerned with what goes on people's heads, but what goes on inside of them."

Vivian makes no pretensions to scholarship. Ask her how she does what she does and she tells you she doesn't really know. "All I know is that I do know--immediately, just like that!" she snaps her fingers for emphasis. "And what I do, I do under a kind of compulsion. How did it come about? How did I discover I had this gift?"

She settles herself in a chair with a cup of coffee, looking at you directly with her gray eyes as she tells her story.

"It happened one night in 1965 in a hotel room in San Francisco. I had been to a lecture by Freedom Barry at the Marines' Memorial Club on Sutter Street and was getting ready for bed when it seemed like a voice inside me said: 'INTERPRET YOUR DAILY LIFE AS YOU DO A DREAM!' When you write this," she broke away, "put that statement in capital letters to emphasize the force with which it came." Then back to her story.

"My immediate reaction was, 'Why, I'm a person who seldom if ever dreams, and certainly without recall. Besides, the interpretation of dreams belongs to God!' At that moment, a dream came back to me that I'd had more than six months before and had forgotten. At the moment the dream returned to me, I had the realization of what it meant. Here is the dream and its interpretation as it came to me:

> "I dreamt I was in a desert. All the way to the horizon the earth was layered with small, loose pebbles. I stood ankle deep in them. It was dusk and I knew I'd have to spend the night there. I had a folded blanket in my hands. 'It

won't be so bad,' I thought, 'I can scoop a trough and spread the blanket under me.' The fading sun was casting shadows and I suddenly realized many people had slept here, for I saw endless troughs, each with a small heap of stones at the head, piled pillow-like, and I thought, 'Oh, they all slept in the wrong direction,' for the rays of the early morning sun would be blinding facing that way. So I decided to turn around and go to sleep in the opposite direction. This dream told me that I had come to that stage of spiritual awakening known as 'repentance.' We've been taught this word means to feel remorse for sin. It means much more. 'Repentance' comes from the Greek word, <u>metanoia</u>, meaning 'to turn around' in one's thinking, to make a radical change of mind toward life. Action follows thought, it does not precede it. The 'desert' symbolized this world we act in. It is an endless expanse of literalness, shown by the complete covering of the ground with pebbles. A 'stone' in the Bible means a literal fact, a truth that is perceived mundanely. While we are 'awake' in life, we sleep amid these small, hard appearances, and the bright sunglare of our senses blinds us into accepting them as total reality. To be ankle deep in stones or pebbles means one's understanding is buried in the shallow truth of this world for the feet symbolize the understanding and shoes or other foot coverings mean literal thinking. Remember what was said to Moses from the burning bush in Exodus? 'Put off thy shoes from off thy feet, for the place whereon thou standest is holy ground.' I discovered all of this while in the dream and made the decision to 'turn around' in the opposite direction. Few symbols depict

41

'death' in dreams better than the desert. My feeling that others had slept there before was correct. But, to me, the dream is always relevant to the one dreaming and what I was seeing in those endless troughs was my endless sleep states, meaning literal thinking, which is like death in comparison to a higher comprehension. That this 'death in sleep states' had ended for me was symbolized by the blanket of enlightened awareness that I held in my hands, separating the ground of literal thinking from that of a more elevated understanding."

At this point Vivian smiled and said, "Later, when I was going through the *Bible,* I found this verse in the Book of Deuteronomy 32:10 'He found him in a desert land, and in the waste howling wilderness; he led him about, he instructed him, he kept him as the apple of his eye.'

"Now," she concluded, "do you see why I say that dreams are living Scripture?"

I said that I did.

Chapter 2

A DREAM IS A REVERSE PARABLE

"Dreams are reverse parables," Vivian told me, "they are stories told to us at night in mental pictures, and we have to convert the images that appear in our dreams into words to understand them."

"To many people dreams are a jumbled mess, just a lot of distortions," I replied, "and not worth trying to understand."

"I know that. And my mission as a dream interpreter is to overcome that feeling. To convince people that dreams are worth trying to understand from the standpoint of our mental, emotional, and spiritual growth."

"Are you successful at it?"

"In a small way, I think so," she said. "Since I first actively began to interpret other people's dreams in 1965, I think I have heard the dreams of maybe three or four hundred persons. Several of them have come back to me often, retaining their interest in dreams for years. And some are doing quite well in probing the most significant symbols that appear in their dreams. It proves I have no monopoly on what I do. What spontaneously awoke in me can be stirred to awaken in others. I am satisfied that it can. If it couldn't, there wouldn't be much point in my doing this work."

"Exactly what do you, and those successful students of yours do, to understand dreams? What are the keys?"

"Well, as I've said, for no reason that I can explain, I know what the symbols that appear in dreams represent and what they mean without much thinking about it, although much more meaning than what at first comes out can be gotten often by probing the dream thoroughly. Ever since I was given the command from within myself, 'INTERPRET YOUR DAILY LIFE AS YOU DO A DREAM,' I have had an instantaneous response to dreams that are told to me. I know immediately what they say--"

"And what do they say?" I broke in.

"They say how well integrated we are on every level of our existence--physical, mental, emotional, and spiritual," she responded, "and our dreams speak to us in the language of symbolism, a language almost completely lost, in spite of the valuable dictionaries of symbols to which we can refer. I say that a dream is a reverse parable. Parables are like dreams in that they contain hidden meanings beyond their literal meanings. They are picture stories. Parables use highly visual words to create dramas in the reader's mind. Are you familiar with what the *Bible* calls The Parable of the Sower?"

"Yes."

"It starts by saying, 'A sower went forth to sow.' That sentence creates a picture. Dreams give us the pictures and we have to convert them into language, into ideas that describe the import of the dream."

"You need keys then," I went back to my question, "to grasp the import?"

"Precisely," she answered, "and those keys are found in Scripture. Two of them are in Genesis: the four rivers that run out of Eden, and the seven days of creation. Both keys are descriptive of Man's consciousness in action. Man is a fourfold being. He exists in physical form, he thinks, and he feels. When he takes thinking and feeling into conviction, it becomes causative. The spiritual level, or mode, of Man's being is this creative or causative quarter."

I then asked about the other key, the seven days of creation.

"Each of these days," she responded, "is a basic aspect of Consciousness, meaning your awareness of being. To know anything you have to be it. Not even God is immune to that. So God, or Consciousness, becomes Man and begins a process of Self-discovery through the activity of these seven basic aspects. This is not original with me.[1] These seven days of creation have been set down by other thinkers as Mind, Principle, Spirit, Soul, Life, Truth, and Love. Through their interplay, all of the experiences of this world are produced. That is what is going on in your dream life, and that is what is going on in your daily life. So I say, as it was said to me, 'INTERPRET YOUR DAILY LIFE AS YOU DO A DREAM.'

---

[1] The idea of the four rivers that run out of Eden, and the idea of the seven days of creation in Genesis, used as a metaphor for seven basic aspects of Consciousness, was introduced to Vivian Heeschen and to the author by a teacher of individual spiritual awakening, Freedom Barry of Cambria, California.

"In my work I correlate colors with these aspects. The color and symbol of Mind is a green tree. Principle is an orange pyramid. Spirit, a white diamond. Soul, a bright star on a purple background. Life, a golden cross. Truth, a blue torch. And Love, a red rose. These symbols show up time without number in the dreams of the people I see. In yours, too, if you pay attention."

"I don't see golden crosses, stars, or blue torches," I said, "but once I had a dream in which I saw a beautiful auburn-haired young woman in a flowing yellow dress. It was covered with a red apron made of the same soft material as the dress."

"You had a marvelous communication," Vivian replied. "The yellow dress of life is covered with the protective red apron of love. The combination of red and yellow produce orange, the symbol color of principle. You must wake to conscious knowledge of actually being Spiritual Identity. That is the principle each of us must grasp--the understanding that whatever you behold is Consciousness garbed in Its own aspects, in eternal delight! You should feel honored to have had such a dream."

"She was indeed beautiful," I said.

"Not she, but you--your soul," Vivian said.

Chapter 3

DREAM AT THE HIGHEST LEVEL

"A dream of the night will yield only that which you have the power to take from it. It will give you no more than you understand," Vivian told me. "If you understand much, you receive much. If you understand little, you receive little. To interpret a dream, you have to be on the level of the dream. You can't see beyond what you yourself are. How we treat our dreams and how our dreams treat us is reflected in this story that might have come from Arabia:

> "A householder found a brass fixture in a rubbish heap and took it home to his wife. Later he asked her what she had done with it. 'Oh, that?' she said, 'I thought it was a worthless thing and threw it out.' 'Foolish woman,' the man muttered, 'all it needed was a new wick and a shade and it would have made a fine lamp.' A second man spied it on the junk pile and took it home. He, too, missed it and when he asked his wife about it, she, too, had discarded it. 'You fool!' he upbraided her, 'it was a rare antique. All it needed was a little polish and I could have sold it for a handsome sum.' A third man then found it and took it home. 'What is it?' his wife asked, 'an antique?

*An old lamp?' 'More than that,' the man said
with excitement, 'it is the lost legendary lamp of
Aladdin!' And together they dwelt in fabulous
comfort.*"

"Like a dream of the night, the man in each
instance represents the mind, that which picks up
impressions. The woman represents the emotions,
that which evaluates. Where a right sense of value
is lacking, no proper judgment can be made, and we
lose much. But where discernment is enlightened,
treasures are delivered to the fortunate possessor."

"I gather you mean spiritual treasure," I said.

She nodded and replied, "We may regard our
dreams and their cryptic messages as priceless heir-
looms, or as leftover trash. 'Unto everyone that
hath shall be given,' says Matthew, 'but from him
that hath not shall be taken away even that which he
hath.'"

I had often wondered what that saying meant.
Now I was beginning to know. Vivian had told me
that God becomes Man and experiences His creation
by the interplay of seven aspects of Consciousness
through four modes of interpreting. God, sleeping
as Man, interprets on three levels: physical, mental,
emotional; and exercising the fourth, or spiritual
mode, mostly unaware, becomes a slave to his convictions that are formed from his beliefs, which he is
forced to experience.

"I can give an example of what happens when
dreams are taken at their lowest level, the level of
literalness," she said. "There comes to mind a
woman who insisted that her dreams always came
true for her. I was explaining to a class that we

shouldn't bring dreams down to a mundane level of interpreting. 'But they do come true for me,' she insisted, 'always!' And she told me a dream she had in which her uncle's leg had been cut off. 'I felt it my duty to warn him, because my dreams always come true,' she said. She believed the Lord wanted her to warn him, with no thought entering her mind that if the Lord wanted to warn her uncle, couldn't He do it? So she telephoned and relayed the message. 'Shortly thereafter,' she said, 'my uncle suffered an accident working on the railroad and his leg was cut off.'

"It's a grave error to take dreams this way. To me, a dream is all about you, and only you, and its message is for you. People who are known to us who appear to us in dreams have something special to say about ourselves because of their closeness, or intimacy. This woman's uncle is a soul symbol. Our legs are what we stand on; they signify our understanding. To lose a leg means to be incapacitated. To be incapacitated in the soul means a faulty sense of evaluation. Taking dreams literally as applying to 'others' is evidence of just such a faulty sense of evaluation. What happens as a result? Her dreams come true because she thoroughly believes it. Her conviction is responsible. What we bring into experience this way is endured for good or bad."

"If that's what you get by taking dreams at their lowest level, what do you get from a higher level?"

"Would you believe peace of mind?" she said.

"I would," I replied.

"I can give an example of how taking dreams literally destroys peace of mind and forces us to live under false assumptions. A middle-aged man told me he had a dream many years ago of finding a dead baby in the trunk of his car. It had such a traumatic effect on him that he said he never bought any kind of car except station wagons, as he did not want to find a dead baby in the trunk. How awful to have to live with that fearful misconception! That isn't what the dream was saying at all! One's car is representative of one's life vehicle, the human body and the human mind. They are machine-like and carry us through life as a car carries us through the world. The dead baby was a symbol of a new growth in the soul, a new life, but it had been stifled by his lack of attention. Not understanding the dream's meaning, he had developed a phobia about owning any kind of car having a trunk. The true function of dreams is to help produce psychic wholeness, to unify us internally, not to give us phobias or frights about others."

Chapter 4

DREAMS TELL US WHERE WE ARE

There is no need for our dreams to disturb us unduly, robbing us of peace of mind, if we understand them. I was convinced of this from talking with Vivian Heeschen, a woman whose intuitive gift is as unique with her as is Jeane Dixon's, or Peter Hurkos'.

"Except that I use my talent to navigate the soul, the dreaming mind, not future events in our world, or the location of missing articles," she said.

She gave me examples of phobias induced by misunderstanding our dreams. "We are prone to take them as implying something about friends, relatives, or other persons who appear in our dreams," she told me. "This is what we are likely to do from having absorbed many of the ideas about dreams that are rampant. But even more so because we are 'asleep' to our true sense of self.

"God asleep as Man interprets physically, mentally, and emotionally. Man awake as God interprets on four levels: physically, mentally, emotionally, and spiritually. Man asleep may believe in God, often he says he does, but he doesn't dare to believe himself to be God. And yet this injunction is shouted at us in Scripture: 'Awake O Sleeper and rise from the dead.' This means to me: 'Cast off your present limited conception of self as one among billions of others populating this globe.' To take the position that you are God asleep as the person whom you know by your name, but destined to awake as Spiritual Identity, as God Himself, requires a radical turn of mind, spoken of in the *Bible* as metanoia.

"If you think that this is all that you are, this organism," Vivian said, touching my forearm, "you are mistaken. The late Alan Watts said that if you are 'awake,' you understand that you are the whole universe projecting itself 'here and now' in the form of a human organism. And you understand that clearly, not just as an idea, but as an actual vivid sensation. I agree with Mr. Watts," she declared.

"Why?" I asked.

"Because, like him, I've experienced it."

"Can you tell me what it was like?"

"Yes. It was a sensation for which the most appropriate word I can think of is 'puddling.' I've never taken LSD, or any of the other so-called 'mind expanding' drugs, but I was sitting alone in my living room meditating one evening when I found that my consciousness was no longer bound by the limits of my physical body. I flowed into everything in the room: sofa, chairs, tables, lamps, windows, drapes, carpets, walls, and ceiling. I could feel the strain of the fabric tacked under the frame of the overstuffed furniture. I felt myself to be the tacks, the tightly stretched fabric. It actually hurt to feel it. I could smell the mustiness of myself as the stuffing. I was the stuffing. I literally was everything to the limit of my horizon, the room in which my body was

52

located. Then I returned to my former sense of self, and the world has been forever different for me ever since. I know what Alan Watts said is true. And it is why I tell my students who come to me for help in knowing their dreams that there is only One Dreamer in all the world, and each human being is that Dreamer. Therefore, all dreams are God's dreams about Himself, identified where you are as the 'you' that you call by your name.

"I know it sounds audacious--and it is. But until we make that turn around, that metanoia, we will continue in the same limited sense of self as we presently are. That is why I am interested in dreams. My dreams. Your dreams. Everybody's dreams. They tell me where The Dreamer is in His sense of Self, whether fast asleep to His Selfhood, thinking Himself to be 'person' among 'persons,' or, in the process of 'awakening,' and just how 'awake' He is."

If that is too much for the average reader--and it is a head-shaker of an idea--at least that is where Vivian is grounded. A good many people who have attended her discussions for a long time say they have reached the same conviction.

An interesting dream was that of a woman who said she had experienced it almost every night for 15 years; a dream in which she invariably woke up crying. "I was about to go out onto the stage with my dancing partner," this woman said, "when I noticed that some part of my costume was missing. Then when I got out onto the stage, my dancing partner, a man, would do the opposite of everything we had rehearsed."

This woman said she hadn't gotten along well with her father in life, and she mistakenly attributed the dream to her relation with him.

"But that wasn't the meaning of the dream to me," Vivian said. "Garments symbolize how we are clothed mentally--what our attitudes are. To be missing a portion of her costume meant that some part of her discernment was missing. Quite true, in that she was bringing her father into it, and he wasn't in it at all! Her dancing partner--a man--in the dream, did everything the opposite of the way they had rehearsed together. He symbolized her soul, her values. He failed her expectations. The dream was saying that her deep unhappiness was due to the impossible demands she was making from life, and life was giving her the opposite of those demands. The dream kept repeating the same theme over and over because she was unable to resolve it satisfactorily and change her attitude.

"When she came to me with the dream, it was having such a bad effect on her that she hated to go to sleep at night. The dream shook her awake in tears. I told her what the dream said to me, and she seemed to accept it. A short time later she came back to me to say that the dream had disappeared. She never had the dream again.

"Our destiny demands that we re-evaluate 'who' and 'what' we think we are, otherwise we tread this plane interminably. We are meant to 'awaken,' but to do so, we have to interpret our dreams at their highest level--spiritually! And we must interpret our daily life as a dream."

Chapter 5

DREAMS TELL US WHERE WE ARE

"To awaken spiritually means to gain a new sense of 'self.' There is but one Self, the substratum of all existence," Vivian said, discussing her dream interpreting. "As William Blake said, 'God is the eternal dreamer dreaming non-eternal dreams.'

"The 'dreamer' is One--Consciousness--playing this three-dimensional planetary theater as 'persons.' When we 'wake' to that fact, to the supreme identification, then the parts that we play on this stage, our roles in life, have been completed. We remain on stage yet awhile to communicate our discovery to those who have not yet made it. That is destiny as I see it," Vivian declared.

"I don't seek to jar humanity out of its doldrums through any cult or organization. I'm not creating a foundation. I represent no religious denomination, creed, or sect, nor do I favor any above others. I don't even go on television much," she laughed as she said it, "some talk show host invariably wants to box me into his format, like trying to get me to admit that dreams foretell our future. They tell our future all right," she went on, "but not in the way most people might think. What they tell us is that if we don't change our attitude about the nature of our being, we'll remain in the same state in which we find ourselves now. That's a pretty hor-rific future, if you ask me, a really grim foretelling! Oscar Wilde said: 'Every person is born a king, but most people die in exile.' That says it.

"On our way to spiritual awakening, dreams can give us some of our most sublime experiences. Why not? If they presage our destiny, then they should have supernal imagery, color, emotion, and meaning, as many dreams do.

"Here is one that is evidence of what I say so many times, that dreams are living Scripture. It is a woman's dream. She had this dream over 20 years ago and hadn't the slightest idea at the time of what it meant. But its emotional impact was so strong that she remembered it all those years and told it to me. It is a dream that is appropriate to what the Western world calls Easter. This is how she told it:

> *"In my dream there were only seven people left in the world, myself and six men, and we had to kill ourselves. One of the men was Jesus and we were all in a rude cabin. I was on the third step of the stairway. Jesus came to me and said it was my turn to commit suicide. He gave me a scissors and told me to plunge it into my heart."*

"This simple dream is filled with meaning. All appearances in this world are made up of the inter-play of seven basic aspects of Consciousness, syn-onymous with the Divine Being. The dream means that God's compound unity is regained by doing away with one's sense of separate appearances, or a separate sense of self. The rude cabin and its seven people represent the whole of the physical universe and its manifestations. To plunge a pair of scissors into one's heart is a symbol of reunion through dissolution, resurrection through death: death of all of what one has previously conceived oneself to be: an independent fragment of being. The scissors represents all paired opposites. The subject's dream demands a piercing of the heart, the organ of life, with one's understanding, likened unto a scissors which is an instrument for severing and separating. To bring pairs of opposites together and to reconcile them is like hinging the blades of a scissors to produce a tool of sharp discernment. And to be told by Jesus to plunge it into one's heart is deliberately to free one's self from one's sense of separateness from Divinity. Finding herself in the dream standing on the third step of the stairway means bringing into unity, as complements, all opposites whether they be physical, mental, or emotional.

"This dream is a variation of the Easter Story. It is my thesis that dreams are living Scripture and here is how the two are related. In the *Bible*, Jesus dies on the cross and is resurrected from the tomb, a story symbolic of the cosmic drama: evolution through involution. Open a pair of scissors until the blades are at right angles and it becomes cross-like in shape and form. Christ, as the living body of humanity, is suspended thereon. Unaware or unawakened to your own divinity, as man or as woman, you are 'hung up' on this cross, this world of opposites which must be harmonized, be reconciled, and brought together like the blades of a scissors, before the two arms of the cross merge into one--before duality can become unity.

"As the heart of Jesus was pierced on the cross by a Roman soldier with a spear, so your heart must be pierced by the understanding of 'who' and 'what' you are before you transcend this life drama. The gesture of Jesus in the dream of handing the woman a scissors means that she must do it herself. It must be a self-inflicted 'death' to a sense of multiplicity, or separateness, well-summarized in the words of a sixteenth century Italian poet, Francesco Berni: 'Everyone must in a measure be alone in the world; for no heart was ever cast in the same mold as that which we bear within us.'

"In conclusion, if you can see that the divine life, living 'as' you, is the only life that you have, then whether Christian or Jew, Turk or Mohammedan, Buddhist or Shintoist, you have brought together, or reconciled the greatest of all seeming opposites: God and Man. To arrive at such an understanding is a piercing of flesh and bone. And from the wound of such piercing flows life eternal for to lose the personal sense of self is to regain Paradise."

Happy Easter, fellow dreamers!

Chapter 6

"Physician, Heal Thyself"

In my discussions with Vivian, I became convinced that the subject of dreams is not the sole province of doctors, psychologists, psychiatrists, or other experts in the workings of the human mind. If any profession deserved to claim a special right to this field of inquiry, it would be the clergy. Except for scattered instances, virtually no church or religious denomination today offers instruction to its members as to the meaning of their dreams, let alone any guide to their understanding.

"We all dream," Vivian said, "so if the dreaming mind is resident in all men, then surely so is the interpretive faculty. But it lies dormant. It has to be enlivened. That's my interest in the subject. To communicate what I understand about dreams in hope that others will conduct their own explorations into their dream lives.

"The secular world has probed dreams about as far as it can. A lot of useful data has been collected. But it's time to look in another direction for the true meaning of dreams. All dreams come from God. Scripture says so. In the Book of Job we read, 'In a dream, in a vision of the night, when deep sleep falleth upon man, in slumberings upon the bed; then he openeth the ears of men and sealeth their instructions.'

"Let me point out," she continued, "that learned researchers, doctors of psychology and psychiatry, stop short in their search for the meaning of dreams. I heard Dr. Ann Faraday, an English dream investigator, discuss her book[2] on KGO radio in San Francisco, on August 21, 1972. Her husband participated with her in the broadcast during which someone called in to ask if two people ever have the same identical dream. 'Yes,' Ann replied. Then she reported in detail a dream that she herself had, and her husband also had on the same night. Here is the dream as she gave it over the air, but she offered the audience no interpretation of it:

> *"In my dream," Ann said, "I found myself in our bedroom. All the furnishings were familiar when to my surprise I discovered a window on the inside wall of the room. After noticing this I looked around at the bed and saw my husband sleeping on the wrong side, so I began to shake him to try to awaken him. Then I awoke from the dream. My husband recounted to me his dream he had the same night and it was identical with mine."*

"This is what I got from Dr. Faraday's dream," Vivian said. "Generally, the dreaming person plays the role of the mind in the dream. The mind receives impressions and takes notice of reports from the five senses. When the mind is glued to the

[2] Ann Faraday, *Dream Power*, [Coward, McCann & Geoghegan, Inc., 1972. Republished by Berkley Medallion, 1980.]

senses it is convinced that the outer objective world constitutes the whole of reality. But this dream shows the dreamer another viewpoint symbolized by the interior window. This window on the inside wall of the bedroom is the insight hidden from the external senses. In Scripture the word metanoia means a radical turning of the mind about self. When this reversal is made, only then does the mind notice that the emotional side of self is asleep on the wrong side of the bed! This emotional side is symbolized as Ann's husband in her dream, and as she, herself, to her husband in his dream. It means in both cases that the dreamer has based reality from the wrong position, or viewpoint. We are not just 'sense-based' creatures. Ann said that in her dream she began to shake her husband to awaken him. In his dream, he did the same to her. Thus the dream for each of them shows that the accepted so-called waking state of sense-based thinking is the sleep of the soul. The intent of this dream that was experienced by Ann Faraday and her husband on the same night, is the attempt to arouse the dreamer to her, and to his, invisible, true identity. The mind must arouse the soul, or emotional side of one's self, to a new orientation of self.

"This leads me to make further comment on many of those who are publicly delving into dreams in our time. It is a good thing, because dreams have been neglected far too long. But some of what I hear as to their conclusions disturbs me. As far as I am concerned, a dream is a report from the Self, to the Self, about the Self--capitalize that, please--but there is a wide range of feeling and understanding about what dreams mean among researchers.

"Why? Because modern dream researchers look at dreams through the filters of borrowed thinking. The intuitive faculty is not operative from the deepest level of discernment. Or else it is clouded by what the interpreter has preconceived as the function of dreams and dreaming from other schools of thought.

"Look at a landscape through a piece of colored glass and everything within view will have that coloration. Say that the glass is yellow. Everything viewed through it will look yellow. Now place a piece of red glass over the yellow glass and look at the landscape again. Everything will look orange, and it will look much darker. Place a piece of blue glass over the red and yellow glass and the world will appear almost black.

"What happens to our view of the objective world when we place glass filters or screens in front of our eyes is what happens to our subjective world of dreams when 'seen' through various 'schools' of dream analysis.

"I look at dreams through none of these filters. I did not learn dream interpreting like you learn accounting, or some school subject. My ability came from no school or college. It 'erupted' in me. It is not my 'person' that is doing it. I see to the depths of dreams and their meaning without any intervening screens of theoretical coloration.

"I did not learn dream interpreting from books. Yet, if you wish, there is a book that contains the keys to the true meaning of dreams. Our *Bible* tells us that the human soul is four-quartered and that the unfolding of conscious understanding, not mere sense-based thinking, takes place in seven stages from obscurity to full illumination.

"There is One Dreamer in all the world dreaming <u>us</u>. Your dream at night is this Dreamer's dream, reported to you in hope that you might know to what degree you recognize yourself as The Dreamer of it all. Dreams are revelations of how buried, or how extracted, The Dreamer is from Its conception of Itself as 'person' or 'one among-seeming-many.'

"It doesn't matter what school of dream theory and practice any researcher or interpreter represents. Until this position is recognized, anybody's guess as to what a dream means is just as good as anybody else's."

"Even mine?" I asked.

"Even yours," she replied.

Chapter 7

INTERPRET YOUR DAILY LIFE

AS YOU DO A DREAM

Dream symbols are from an ancient forgotten language, crusted over by our dependence on spoken and written words. Before written language evolved, men used pictographs to communicate ideas. Alphabets have since replaced pictographs. The ancient language of symbolism has been obscured. But your deep Self has not forgotten this language. It weaves dreams of dramatic structure out of universal symbols, often including symbols that are highly personal to you, and charges your dreams with emotion to force their memory into your waking state.

"I'll tell you what dreams are," Vivian said. "Dreams are God talking about Himself, to Himself, in the language where He is keyed as your person. Isn't that a beautiful philosophy?"

"And beautifully stated," I said.

"Sometimes," she said, "the language whereby He speaks to one of us has meaning for us all. It always does, but some dreams are more pointedly so. Take a dream of a man I know employed as a technical writer. He said he dreamt of a small town that had only one through street. A stop light at an intersection stayed red for two hours. He found himself driving toward this intersection when the light changed from green to red. He had three alternatives. (1) He could take a long, twisting detour around the town; (2) He could sit it out at the intersection until the light changed to green again; or (3) He could go back home. What should he do? He awoke wondering which alternative to take.

"We all have the same three choices," she went on. "The small town represents a mental construction, the literal world in which we find ourselves. The street intersection is a horizontal union where traffic moving in different directions comes together. It stands for the connection of thinking [green light] and feeling [red light], whose influences alternate in directing our lives. The 'long, twisting detour' is the labyrinth of all the possible states of experience one can enter and follow in this life. To make that choice is a long trip. To 'sit it out for two hours' means to assume a static position in this world of duality, symbolized by the number 'two,' It means to serve nature, or remain as a function of nature, and let one's fate be determined by the automatic changes that come in time. The best choice would be to 'go back home' for that is <u>metanoia</u>, a radical turning about in one's conception of oneself.

"I'll give you another example of a dream pointed to all of us," Vivian said. "Life is a movement in growth and experience from one state of consciousness to another. We pass from state to state as we rise. This transmigration is the evolution of the soul, and Scripture is its chronicle. In 1st Corinthians 15:22 we read: 'For as in Adam all die, even so in Christ shall all be made alive.' Scripture is thus really your biography and should be read as such.

"A California woman had a dream in which she saw a large *Bible,* and running across the bottom of it was a line of type that read: 'THE STORY OF EVERYMAN. . . WITH DRAMATIC OVERTONES.' While she looked at it in her dream, an unseen voice whispered to her, 'To help sell the book!'

"This universe and all that is in it is nothing but God experiencing His own creation. As William Blake said, 'Eternity is in love with the productions of time.' To experience Itself, It must forget Itself, first falling asleep as Man--Adam, and then rousing Itself to rediscover Its divinity--Christ. That is all that is going on in our three-dimensional world, and that is all that is going on in our dream world at night. We must therefore, learn to interpret our daily life as we do a dream.

"Dreams are trying to say the same thing to you that the parables and allegories of Scripture are saying--'awake.' Our Scriptures were written long ago, its authors mostly forgotten, but your dreams are current with your life and time, here and now. I meet people whose dreams have direct references to Scriptural passages. And because dreams report to us whether we are progressing or standing still, not being able to understand your dreams is like not being able to read your bank statements. You don't know how much you have on deposit.

"The reason we don't understand our dreams is that we have forgotten how to think symbolically. Universal symbols are unrecognized in dreams for often they appear as 'lead' characters in the dream who bear a waking-life relationship to us. Thus we think of these characters in the dream story as representing themselves, whereas they are depicting some of our own characteristics. For example, a woman's images of 'feeling' are portrayed as masculine when she dreams. The opposite is true for a man. His 'feeling' images are feminine. With some qualification, however. The meaning of dream symbols lies in what the dream itself is telling us through the relationships and actions of the characters. 'Relatives' are close relationships of our identified states of mind and feeling. Friends and neighbors also carry the same implication. Children, our own or others, often mean new formulations, or undeveloped ones, the beginning of new concepts and expressions in the depth of Self.

"So a woman should know that in her dream life her feeling nature can appear as her husband, brother, uncle, cousin, or male neighbor or friend. In a man's dream life his feeling nature is presented as his wife, sister, aunt, cousin, or female neighbor or friend. To either gender, feelings sometime appear as a stranger, one who is unknown.

"The human father of the dreamer, whether man or woman, is always symbolic of 'The Father of Creativity,' the dreamer's Eternal Being: unconditioned, unlimited Consciousness. The human mother of the dreamer symbolizes Mother Nature, the dreamer's personal sense of self. The mother of any dreamer, man or woman, signifies all that the dreamer has acquired and built up about himself through life experience. The mother figure is the ruler, one's personality. An example from literature is the story of Snow White. She represents the Eternal Identity, Consciousness, subjugated by the wicked queen who consults her mirror: the mask, the entrenched 'persona' we let rule.

"When your dream shows the departure of 'lead' characters by your seeing them dead or dying, this signifies something about the dormant side of Self: your change and alteration with the passing on of these familiar characters in the dream. It is you the dream is talking about, not these 'others,' as 'people' to be reckoned with when you are in your wakened state.

"There comes to mind a dream by a man of mature years who wrote to me: 'I was holding a tiny baby and it hugged me and loved me and I felt the same toward it. A woman stood near. She was faceless and said, 'It's no good. It's neither male nor female. Get rid of it.' To me it was precious. It loved me and I loved it.'

"The baby is a symbol of the Spiritual Identity, helpless and fragile. The faceless woman is the dreamer's persona, the pseudo-self--faceless--with no reality to it. It is what the dreamer thinks he is and he wishes to continue relating to that concept of himself by destroying the true concept of Self. The baby is the dreamer's soul and needs care in the infantile stage of growing and expanding to full Consciousness. The dreamer, by willing to change position in the depths of himself and recognizing Consciousness as 'cause,' not persona, can aid the awakening from the sense of being finite, separated 'person,' to the infinite One."

Chapter 8

INTERPRET YOUR DAILY LIFE

AS YOU DO A DREAM

Dreaming Man in our Western world is locked into a critical situation today, for he gets little help from the church on the religious significance and understanding of dreams. And the interest of the secular world seems largely limited either to the mechanics of sleep and dreams by charting eye movements, and how long and how often they occur while sleeping, or to the elusive attempt to relate telepathy to dreams. In controlled experiments, attempts are made to pass thoughts from the mind of a waking person into one who is asleep and then garner proof of it by comparing the sleeper's recall of dream images with the images that the experimenter was attempting to pass to him.

But as Morton Kelsey says in his book, *Dreams: The Dark Speech of the Spirit*[3] "--we will wait a long time for our consciousness to start catching up with the wisdom of God if we ignore the dream that has personal religious significance and sit around waiting for an ESP experience."

---

[3] Morton T. Kelsey, *Dreams: The Dark Speech of the Spirit.* [Doubleday, New York].

Nonetheless, intelligent men keep trying to pass ideas from the heads of ESP experimenters into those of dreamers. To what purpose and end?

If a man at a distance from another man happens to dream of tomato plants at the same time as the other man was thinking about them, of what value is it? If I can make you think of a tomato plant, or a rosebud, while you sleep, so what?

When I put these questions to Vivian she smiled as though enjoying some private joke saying, "If you don't mind, I'll take the tomato plant over the rosebud. The tomato is called the 'love apple,' you know. But to be serious, though I don't like to generalize about dream symbols, the greenness of the tomato plant stands for the aspect of Mind, and its ripe, red fruit represents the aspect of Love; recall what I said about the seven basic aspects of Consciousness."

"I do recall," I said.

"The meaning of dream symbols lies in the context of the dream," she continued, "which is why dream dictionaries are of no real help in getting at the meaning of dreams--"

"Then you put no stock in them?" I broke in.

"Not the least. The descriptions are arbitrary. But the number of such books sold is evidence of what widespread interest people have in their own dreams, and how hungry and starved they are for knowledge as to their meaning.

"A woman of my acquaintance who worked in an art gallery had a dream in which a voice said: 'PAINT THE COAST OF CALIFORNIA WITH A

BELL!' How could she get meaning from a dream like that by consulting a dream book?"

"I don't see much meaning in it, dream book or no dream book," I said.

"No? It's a great dream, as they all are. Particularly, when someone speaks and you don't see who it is. It's the voice of Conscience. It told this woman she had something important to do. 'Paint the coast of California with a bell.' California is her home state. It is also known as the Mission State because of the mission trail along its coastline founded by Father Junipero Serra. So she has a 'mission.' To refurbish the inner state of her mind and emotions with better thoughts and moods."

"How do you arrive at that?"

"By asking myself, what do 'paint' and 'bell' have in common? They both produce colorful tones. Colors from a paint brush reach the mind through the eye, while the tones of a bell reach us through the ear. The eye to me is a Mind symbol. The ear is a Soul symbol. She is being told to re-tone her mental and emotional world, to change her conception of herself."

"We've talked at length about what it means to see our father and mother, our relatives and friends, in our dreams," I reminded her. "We also talked about colors. What are some other symbols that occur often?"

"Numbers," she replied. "There is a process of inner assembly, or reunification, going on all the time, of which we are unaware, until our waking consciousness is closed down in sleep. Then we receive progress reports in this direction toward the goal of unification, or Oneness, signified by the number '10.' The zero is for emphasis, Oneness to infinity. The tenth letter of the Hebrew alphabet is 'Yod.' It signifies the Absolute. It signifies the 'power' of unconditioned Consciousness.

"I said before that the numbers 'one' through 'seven' stand for each of the seven basic aspects of Consciousness which have been ordered by some thinkers as Mind, Principle, Spirit, Soul, Life, Truth, and Love. Numbers show up in dreams in many ways. Often we see them written just as we do in our waking life. Sometimes they are represented by quantities or measurements. I can give you a good example.

"A man had a dream that told me a lot about his inner development. 'I dreamt of a large book,' he said. 'Its title was on the cover in large, all-white capital letters: "The Life of Ecstasy." It also had a price tag marked $4.95.'

"To interpret his dream, I added all the numbers: four, plus nine, plus five, totalling 18. Adding the 'one' and 'eight' of 18, gives 'nine,' signifying 'The Kingdom of Heaven,' the state of being conscious Man as contrasted with sleeping Man whose number is 'six,' the number of Adam. Genesis says he was created on the 'sixth day,' remember?

"Numbers on the left and right of decimal points give finer meanings. I regard the number on the left as the solution to the situation implied by the number on the right. In the sum of $4.95, 'four dollars' means the unification of the four quarters of the human soul, which is achieved by interpreting

74

life from four perspectives rather than three, which is how Adam, or sleeping Man, interprets.

"The figures on the right of the decimal point, 'nine' and 'five,' add to 14, which reduces by addition to 'five.' Five, of course, is the familiar fifth aspect of Consciousness: Life. To me, this dream is telling the dreamer that totally awakened Consciousness, and the achievement of it, is the 'price' of 'The Life of Ecstasy.'"

Chapter 9

INTERPRET YOUR DAILY LIFE

AS YOU DO A DREAM

"Tell me more about 'sleeping Man' and 'conscious Man,'" I said to Vivian.

"We were discussing numbers, how they show up in our dreams, and what they signify," she responded. "Our Scriptures are filled with descriptions of psychological states that range all the way from the lowest degree of Self-awareness, that of Adam, or 'sleeping Man,' to the highest degree of Self-awareness, that of Christ, or 'conscious Man.' These opposing states are characterized as the 'quick' and the 'dead.' Until we 'awaken' as Christ, the power and wisdom of God active on earth, we are 'dead,' spiritually speaking. We live as Adam, naming the 'beasts of the field,' as described in Genesis, meaning classifying all of our perceptions and impressions as though we had independent life and volition. The indwelling Christ lies dormant, and remains so until we experience 'rebirth,' symbolized by an infant, a babe.

"Intimations of this come to us in our dreams and in our waking life as well. But most of us are so ignorant of the spiritual significance of these events that we can't always appreciate what is taking place within us. Almost always, however, dreams in which a heralding of spiritual rebirth is dramatized are communicated with striking imagery and emotion, so that a memory of these dreams stays with us. Remember the dream I told you of the man who found a dead baby in the trunk of his car?"

I nodded.

"And that of another man who dreamt he was holding and hugging a tiny baby when a faceless woman told him to get rid of it?"

I nodded again.

"Well, here's a case where I have to take back what I said about a man's dream revealing his soul, or his feeling nature, as a female figure. She is 'faceless,' meaning she represents persona, a mere mask, which has no permanence. But let's get back to the subject of numbers."

She handed me a pencil and a tablet of paper. Draw an Arabic numeral '6,'" she said. I did so. "Now describe for me what you did," she said.

"Well, I started with a point and drew a curving line downward in a counter-clockwise direction that ended in a closed loop."

"Good. Now can you see that if you had continued to draw, you would be making an ever-tightening inward spiral with the pencil?" I could see that. "Now I want you to draw me an Arabic numeral '9,'" she said. I drew one for her alongside the '6.' "That's good," she said. "Tell me what you did this time."

"I made a loop starting with a curving line upward in a clockwise direction, and when I closed the loop I left a short stem at the bottom."

"You can see," she pointed as she traced my '9' with her fingernail, "that if you had kept on drawing, you would have made an expanding, outward spiral?"

"Yes," I agreed.

"That's how I see this cosmic drama," she said, "in which our present focus is that of numerous separate players, who are born, strut briefly on-stage, and depart. It's a marvelous scheme of evolution through involution. This earth of ours is the limit of contraction for Consciousness. You can't get any farther down than this, the state of Adamic man, symbolized by the number '6.' All you can do is proceed upward--or stay where you are," she added, "if you don't become aware of Who and What you are in essence: God in embryo.

"The number '9' represents expansion, 'The Kingdom of Heaven,' or as the late Dr. Maurice Nicoll,[4] a British pioneer in psychological medicine called it: 'the circle of conscious humanity.'

"Now lets take the '6' and the '9' and erase the stems," she said doing it, "and what do we have?"

"Two circles," I said.

She drew two circles joined and made a figure '8.' "When you turn the number '8' on its side, it becomes the mathematical symbol for infinity. In music, the eighth note of a scale repeats the note that began it, making an octave--a completion and a new beginning. In dreams it stands for Christhood-- a new ascension in consciousness. Sleeping Man, or Adam--number 'six'--is bridged to the circle of

---

[4] Maurice Nicoll, *Psychological Commentaries on the Teachings of Gurdjieff and Ouspensky.* [Vincent Stuart, London, 1957. Volumes I-V.]

conscious humanity--number 'nine'--through Christ--number 'eight'--through the office of Love, whose number is 'seven,' spiritual perfection.

"Is there anything else you would like to talk about?" Vivian asked. "That's about as far as I go with numbers in dreams."

"Tell me what it means," I said, "if you dream of famous or important people. Presidents. Movie stars. Or other celebrities."

"About what you might expect. Something important in the way that Consciousness sees Itself and reports it. Can you give an example?"

"I know someone who dreams of Eisenhower a lot. What does he mean?"

"Is it a man?"

"Yes."

"Was he in the army?"

"Yes."

"When Eisenhower was?"

"Yes. World War II."

"Ike Eisenhower was commander-in-chief in Europe."

"This was in Paris at SHAEF. Supreme Headquarters of the Allied Expeditionary Forces."

"Then that's what he is in the dream. The Chief. The Supreme Self."

"He met him in a dream in a house belonging to actress, Ann Baxter--"

"She's the granddaughter of the great architect, Frank Lloyd Wright."

"She is?"

"Yes."

"I wasn't aware of that. Anyway, the house was beautiful. A long, low ranch-style house."

"All on one level, a sign of unity."

"The house was worth $160,000."

Vivian beamed at me. "Great."

"In the dream, that is."

"I understand. Six and one make seven. The structure of divine Love. Frankly, what could be more 'right' than that?"

"You're punning, Vivian."

"Me? Dreams do it all the time."

"They do?"

"You have a lot to learn. Keep dreaming. You'll be a collector."

"And this fellow met Eisenhower in Ann Baxter's living room," I went on.

"The residence of the Soul."

"And Miss Baxter was there, too."

"The Soul is always in residence with the Supreme."

"And he said he couldn't get over seeing Eisenhower so alive. He knew that Eisenhower had died a few months before. He was thinking about this, marvelling about it in the dream that Eisenhower was alive and talking to him. So he said to him, 'What are you going to do now, General?' And Eisenhower replied, 'I'm going to lead an orchestra.' To which he said, 'Then I'll lead a trio.'"

Vivian was amused at all this. "Is that it?"

"That's it."

"What a rich dream! The dreamer is housed in Love's construction with the unified Mind and Emotions. The supreme occupation is to orchestrate harmony. And this he does by integrating the per-forming trio, the three modes of interpreting while he is identified in the role of physical, mental, and emotional man."

Vivian's eyes were sparkling. "Who was it who wrote that song? 'My Dreams Are Getting Better All the Time.' I'll say to you like I say to my students. Every time you tell me a dream it belongs to me. I add it to my Self-knowledge."

Chapter 10

SEX AND THE DREAMER

"I'll bring up a subject for dream interpretation that you haven't mentioned," Vivian said.

"All right, what is it?"

"Sexual seduction," she replied.

"Well, you brought it up. Let's have it," I said.

"The world owes a great deal to Freud for his pioneer work in dreams," she began, "he opened up a gate that Aristotle closed. But, as Jung and others found, Freud left much to be resolved satisfactorily when it comes to sexual expressions in dreams. I am thinking of an article in one of the major women's magazines in which the author, a woman, was discussing male impotence. She wanted to point out that it has an old history, so she mentioned that in the *Bible* young Joseph was nearly seduced by an Egyptian woman whose husband was impotent. It is all right for authors to draw upon any sources they choose for examples upon which to make points, but I deplore the ignorance that is manifest when a Scriptural incident connotes nothing more than its literal meaning to the reader.

"What do you see in it?" I asked.

"To me, it typifies in an intimate way how much our dreams and our lives are 'living Scripture.' People often hesitate to discuss freely dreams in which they have intimate relations with persons other than their spouses. They feel they reveal guilty desires. Now whether a person should feel a sense of guilt for dreams of infidelity, only his conscience can say. I have no desire to be anyone's conscience. I know it is dangerous to generalize, but many dreams of intimate sexual relations are really those of soul unification with the new man, or the new woman, the dreamer is becoming psychically, and are not necessarily correlated positively with a person's behavior in waking life, or secret desires for such affairs.

"Let's go back to young Joseph in the *Bible*. Who and what was he? He was one of Jacob's youngest sons who was sold into slavery in Egypt by his brothers because his father had given him a 'coat of many colors.' In Egypt he had to serve Pharaoh. Joseph had a gift for understanding dreams and he warned Pharaoh of famine in the land through a dream of Pharaoh's that no one but he could interpret. As a result, he won Pharaoh's respect and was elevated to a high station in Egypt.

"But first, Joseph was owned by Potiphar, the captain of Pharaoh's guard, who bought him from the Ishmaelites, and made him the overseer of his household. Potiphar's wife, the Egyptian woman who tried to seduce Joseph, symbolizes the soul. You, whether you are man or woman, are Joseph. You are dwelling as a slave in Egypt, for Egypt is the world of spiritual darkness in which all men are sent to dwell. But you have an innate gift that came with you into slavery. It is your dormant, intuitive faculty that has power to interpret dreams as well as your 'waking' experience in this world on a psychological, or spiritual basis. When that faculty is roused and becomes active, it earns the respect of Pharaoh, the sense-based mind, and raises you spiritually. Pharaoh, or <u>persona</u>, instead of operating as ruler in the psyche, becomes merely a 'front man' for Joseph, the power of one's awakened imagination.

"When the 'new man' in you is being generated in Potiphar's house, you, as this 'new man,' become attractive to the soul who wishes to unify with you.

"Now we come to a serious untruth by the author of the magazine article I'm talking about, for she said that the Egyptian woman's husband was impotent. But there isn't one word of that in the Biblical story. Read it in Genesis 39:7-20. You won't find any reference to Potiphar's impotence.

"Recall what we discussed earlier, how when a man dreams, his feeling side, or soul, appears as a female other than the mother. When a woman dreams, the converse is true. Her feeling nature, or soul, is depicted by a male figure other than the father.

"To show you our ignorance of what dreams are trying to say, I am reminded of a woman who told me that one night while she lay asleep in bed with her husband, he had a dream in which she appeared drunk and was going to go off with some other men. He shouted and screamed at her in his dream not to do it, but she did it anyway. When he awoke in the morning, he berated her for her infidelity <u>in his dream</u>! The dream was not about her. It was all about him, as all dreams are always about the one who is having them.

"For him to have seen his wife drunk means that his soul, his emotional or feeling nature, is inebriated with all the occupations of this our waking world. His soul has no 'will' of its own, and goes off with, or yields to, every impression and influence that comes along, here personified in the dream as strange men, meaning 'mentations.'

"Without knowing the man better," Vivian concluded, "I would hazard a guess that his soul is searching for spiritual satisfaction in externals because he is denying its needs within himself. But in his ignorance and smugness, he projected what the dream was trying to tell him onto the person of his wife.

"Every dream is always a communication to the subject about himself. But not knowing better, he reduces it to baser considerations."

Chapter 11

SEX AND THE DREAMER

In discussing sex and the dreamer with Vivian, I recalled some psychoanalytic theory: that dreams represent a compromise between unexpressed sexual or aggressive urges and the moral attitudes that censor them.

To which she said, "All of life is a constant battle between the constructive and the destructive forces within Man, so there is an element of truth in that, for as William James declared, 'If this life be not a real fight in which something is eternally gained for the universe by success, it is no better than a game of private theatricals from which one may withdraw at will.' But I do not agree that dreams are just a mode of disguising hostilities and sex impulses that have been repressed. That doesn't constitute the all-in-all of dreaming, nor are those elements necessarily disguised. Freud himself was disturbed by his fellow psychoanalysts who accepted without critical examination the ideas he formulated and went overboard with them. He said that they behaved 'as though the whole subject of dream theory were finished and done with.'

"From his speculations, they went off on a tangent, to the point where someone has defined a psychologist as a man trying to catch a black cat in a dark alley at midnight, and a psychoanalyst as the same fellow--except there's no cat there."

I laughed at that. "Then you turn thumbs down on Freud?"

"No, I didn't say so. I don't imply it. It's what psychoanalytical theory did to Freud's work. In his autobiography Freud said, 'I have never maintained the assertion, which has so often been ascribed to me, that dream interpretation shows that all dreams have a sexual content or are derived from sexual motive forces.'

"I am asked often about sex dreams. They distress many because of the fact Freud advanced the concept of repressed sexuality emerging in dreams. I wish to start no argument with present-day Freudians but I will quote a verse from Piet Hein's little book, *Grooks*, published by Doubleday:

Dream Interpretation Simplified

Everything's either
Concave or--vex
So whatever you dream
Will be something with sex.

How true! The Freudian concept deals in duality, the play of opposites, when in reality dreams of union between the sexes frequently connote wholeness of The Dreamer by the fusion of 'mind' (male) and 'emotion' (female). As I say, generally, the emotional nature of a man who dreams is represented in them as 'woman,' while the emotional nature of a woman who is dreaming is signified by 'man.' It is not necessarily true, as some have said, that women's dreams of sexual relations concern male partners known to them, nor that when men dream of sexual congress with women that the women are strangers to them. Men may often say that it's a stranger because that may be more accurate. Gentlemen, too, hide truth."

We talked again, briefly, of the man who awoke in the morning and berated his wife for what he considered her unseemly conduct with other men in his dreams.

Vivian said, "If our dreams reprove us, as this man's dream reproved him--not her--it is because we are deserving of it. But God doesn't hate anybody. How could He when He's here as everybody? It is from within our sleep, the loss of the knowledge of who and what we are, that we must rouse ourselves.

"Of course, sex dreams can signify a whole range of things from spiritual unification to the depths of debasement and perversion. What the dream tells the one who is having it is where he is polarized. From gross sexual appetite and servile passion to the heights of divine rapture, dreams reflect the gamut of all human possibility and experience. Shakespeare said that 'we are such things as dreams are made on,' but I say the reverse is also true. Dreams are such things as we are made on."

Chapter 12

DREAMS BELONG IN CHURCH

Carl Gustav Jung decided over and against Sigmund Freud that it is unnecessary to use dreams as starting points for "free associations" to uncover a patient's complexes. He held that dreams have more significant functions of their own. Consequently he concentrated on the dreams themselves.

"That goes for me, too," Vivian said during our discussion. "I attend only to the dream and its own contents. I try to keep my students focused in the same way. The meaning is in the dream content, and not in the associations that trail off from it."

"But medical practitioners," I reminded her, "often use dreams and free associations to try and get at a patient's repressed thoughts and desires."

"Certainly," she replied. "They're welcome to do that, if they wish. But to me, to use dreams in such a way while ignoring what they mean on a spiritual level is like using a jeweled comb for a screwdriver. Why ignore the most exalted function of dreams to look for signs of neurotic disturbances in them? Word association tests will do just as well for that purpose. But I don't argue with psychoanalysts or psychiatrists on what they do to their patient's dreams. That's their business. I'd like to see everyone who has an interest in dreams come up a little higher in their evaluation of them, especially theologians. Churchmen today are derelict, in my opinion, in not concerning themselves with the dreams of the members of their parishes and congregations, for they spell out the relationship of the dreamer to God in the most intimate way."

"How do you think the churches should go about doing this?"

"Well, with so many ecumenical movements, it seems to me that forming an interfaith council to make a special study of dreams and the religious needs of men would be one way of strengthening such movements."

"Have you ever thought of offering that idea to any church body?"

"No, but now that you've brought it up, maybe what we've been discussing in these interviews will reach the attention of some church leaders who will take that initiative."

"You don't feel like taking it yourself, with what you know about the spiritual meaning of dreams?"

Her response was a shake of the head. "Spiritual awakening is an individual process and I find that personal counseling and instructing small groups is more in keeping with my temperament rather than trying to rally all Christendom. It would take a lot of travelling. I'm not one to organize. I speak to small groups within churches but I don't try to bring leaders of diverse faiths together. It's not my talent. And it would be difficult even for someone with a lot of high powered executive ability. Much of what dreams say does violence to church dogma. Churches have ignored the vast subject of dreams for centuries. How could any layman, such as I, overcome that inertia?"

"If you could make one clear statement to the churches about man's spiritual condition as you see it through dreams, what would it be?"

"Let me see--" she paused. "There are many things I could say, and I've said a lot of them during our talks. I would say the majority of the dreams of most people are what I call 'lost in life' dreams. The Dreamer, dreaming it all, is shut down as <u>persona</u> to the divine sense of Itself, until It 'wakes.' I'd like to tell you some dreams that show that."

"Please do," I urged.

"A man had a dream in which he saw his mother alone in a boat. She fell overboard into the water, and before the dreamer could help her, he awoke." She stopped and looked at me.

"Well?" I said.

"Well, what?" she replied. "That says it all, as condensed as you can put it. The Eternal Dreamer is Consciousness, or Spiritual Identity, which enters into all forms of nature, personified by the dreaming man's mother. Spiritual Identity, as the creative matrix or mother of all things, leaves the boat, the 'ark,' or vessel of Self-containment, and plunges voluntarily into the water, the undifferentiated sea of life. The dreaming man witnessed what happened to his mother but he did not see his personal sense of self as a separate entity with her in the boat, for Spiritual Identity commits Itself, as 'mother,' and takes the plunge into the potentiality of creation, the ocean of all conceivable possibilities, and does not attempt to 'save' Itself, or retract Its own willed action. The Scriptures say, 'My word shall not return unto me void.' 'My word shall not turn back until it accomplishes that unto which it is sent.' The Eternal Dreamer is 'The Word,' or meaning made manifest, and sends Itself into this world of physical forms to enrich Itself. Having done so, It extracts Itself from the world with all of Its acquired experience."

"That says it all," I said.

"Doesn't it, though? Can you understand what a thrill it is to me when I hear a dream like that? A dream doesn't have to be long to be comprehensive, or deeply meaningful. Here's another dream by the same man, almost like it. He said that he dreamt his father-in-law was on the ground floor of a building, and the second floor crumbled and fell upon him. His father-in-law called out, 'Oh, what have I done that this should happen to me!' He said he was above his father-in-law and reached down and took him by the arm, and then awoke.

"Here again, Spiritual Identity, this time identified as 'father-in-law,' descends or 'falls' from Its polarity of infinity into the world of finite being. In his other dream, his 'mother' embraces all forms to enliven or give warmth to them, an act that typifies the emotional and feeling nature of Consciousness. The 'father-in-law' personifies creativity, the mental nature of Consciousness. The aspect of Consciousness as Principle, the second floor, is seen collapsing because mental constructions have no independent reality of their own. The cry, 'Oh, what have I done that this should happen to me!' calls forth the cry of

94

Jesus from the cross in Scripture, 'My God, my God, why hast thou forsaken me!' To give up the divine sense of Self in order to live as Man, is like unto a state of total amnesia while in this state. Divinity has forgotten who It is while affixed to Its finite identifications. It's your state of amnesia, whether you are the man who had the dream or not. But Spiritual Identity retains the power to rescue Itself from all Its mentations as expressed by the action of the one dreaming in grasping the father-in-law by the arm. The grasp is made by the hand, a symbol of power, and the arm represents extended understanding. The act of rescue is that of the 'son-in-law.' A son is one's issue, present to oneself as a reminder of being a father. The relation here is that of father-in-law and son-in-law, they are bound by the same principle, signifying their similarity, their likeness of nature. That which is 'present' is the previously held sense of Self as divine, making Its own rescue from Its creation. To do so is to regain the lost perspective, to be 'resurrected from the dead,' meaning his world of duality and its play of opposites."

Chapter 13

DREAMS BELONG IN CHURCH

Vivian handed me a folder labelled "Parables of the Soul." "These," she said, "are a few classic dreams from my collection." She turned to one titled "The Ghastly Ship." It belonged to a man who had been in the Navy:

"I and several other people I cannot picture in my world," he had written, *"got a used vessel about the size of a sea-going tug, which is a fair size. We worked hard to shape it up, cleaning, repairing, and polishing it on the outside. Then someone said, 'Your wife is dead.' I and the crew expected it. 'She was in charge of cleaning the inside of the ship,' I said, 'let's look and see what she has done.' We removed the hatch cover and peered into the hold. What I saw was a frightful shock to me. Nothing had been done. It was like opening a tomb a thousand years old. Nothing was stacked properly. Dust and cobwebs covered everything. It was so ghastly I wouldn't go down into it and try to clean it up. 'This is the end,' I then thought. 'The vessel is sunk.'"*

"I know this man well," Vivian said. "Years ago in a vision he had he was told, 'You are going to die when you are 45.' He is past 45 and he isn't dead, not physically. What was meant was the death of the soul. Small wonder to me that he should have a dream like this.

"The dreamer and the party of people unknown to him represents Consciousness and Its functions. The ship is the Soul, the essence of Consciousness. All the effort in cleaning it is expended on external appearances. Like the Pharisees of old whom Jesus reproves in the Gospel of Matthew, he is making clean 'the outside of the cup,' while inside he is 'full of hypocrisy and iniquity.'

"This state is typical of humanity where Consciousness is asleep to Its divinity. The 'dead wife' stands for the deadness, the inertness, of the Soul, unable to perform any interior cleansing. The capacity for Self-redemption at this time is lifeless as shown by the dreamer's remark, 'This is the end. The vessel is sunk.' The 'ship' is the dreamer and with no inner arousal it can't be raised, or salvaged.

"Every time I refer to that dream," she said, "it sends a chill through me. Now let's consider another dream similar but not quite so repulsive. It is a woman's dream:

> *"My son came to visit me in this dream and asked if he could borrow my shampoo. I went and got it and gave it to him. He said, 'Thank you, I'm going to drink it,' as he uncapped the bottle. I said, 'That's crazy. I'm going to talk to my doctor about you.' So I phoned the doctor and told him my son's intentions. He said, 'Let him do as he wills.' And I woke up."*

"The dreamer being a woman, her feeling nature is represented as masculine. Her son is the Soul. His desire to drink the shampoo represents the intention of Spiritual Identity to cleanse Itself from Its impurities, meaning Its misconceptions, thinking of Itself as persona.

"Let's compare the two dreams. The ex-Navy man's dream tells us that we are slow to recognize our divinity. Truly, the Pharisee is in us all for we are so busy shaping up the exterior of life, trying to make conditions more pleasant for persona, that we neglect the most important duty. We think the life of the flesh is our only reality. In this dream the true work of the Soul has not even begun, for note the reference to the inner disorder as having existed for 'a thousand years.'

"In the woman's dream, at least there is an intention of Soul cleansing, even if unbeknown to the surface mind of the dreamer. The Soul, represented as her son, wants cleansing and will do it Itself.

"In the Navy man's case, there is the knowledge within him that his soul is lifeless, for at the announcement, 'Your wife is dead,' he admitted, 'I and the crew,' meaning all the mental sides of himself, 'expected it.'"

Vivian leafed over a few more pages in her file folder. "When it comes to 'lost in space' dreams, here's a gem. It's the dream of an elderly woman but it's a universal dream.

"She dreamt she was lying in bed when she was called to the telephone in an adjacent room. She rose and as she did so, she noticed that her bedroom was empty of all furnishings except for the bed

99

upon which she had been lying. She had charge of two, small oriental boys and they followed her out of the bedroom and into the other room where the phone was. But as she approached a built-in shelf, she saw there was no phone there. Where the wall should have been was nothing but empty space. There was nothing to see but sky. It was dusk. There was no earth. No stars. Just sky. The children were whimpering and the woman's daughter, who seemed to be 14 years old, quieted the children. One of the boys said sadly, 'My father is lost in space.' The dreamer replied, 'That's all right. Don't be concerned. He can never make a mistake.'

"Isn't that a great dream?"

"If you say so."

"It is. It's about 'inner space,' the atmosphere of the Soul. The dreamer is asleep in the barren 'room' of life--this world of ours--when she is called to communicate with something else, symbolized by the 'telephone' in the 'adjacent room.' The 'two small oriental boys' represent the Orient, noted for ancient wisdom and understanding. The fact that there is no 'phone' means that the dreamer cannot find a connection with a higher level of being even though she perceives the vastness of space. The 'two children,' her undeveloped soul faculties of wisdom and understanding, are in distress for they are whimpering. The dreamer's 'daughter,' although in reality older than '14,' is shown to her as 14. This is significant for it reveals the dreamer's mental functions are based on the reality of the literal world. 'Four' and 'one' are 'five,' the Life aspect of Consciousness. The mind quells the children's despair and when one boy says, 'My father is lost in space,' he is telling the dreamer that she is unconnected with her Spiritual Identity. The Father, Consciousness Itself, is lost to Its own nature when identified as 'person.'

"This dream correlates with a New Testament verse, the Second Epistle of Peter, chapter 3, verse 4." She opened a *Bible* on her coffee table and read it: "'Where is the promise of his coming? For since the fathers fell asleep, all things continue as they were from the beginning of creation.'

"It's an eternal progression," she said with a sweeping motion toward her open window. "The promise is fulfilled to us, who are the 'fathers,' but only after a long journey through this desert-like world."

Chapter 14

FAMILIES SHOULD

DISCUSS THEIR DREAMS TOGETHER

When all is said, each of us should learn to be his own dream interpreter. Even gifted dream interpreters, such as Vivian Heeschen, who offer guidelines to the spiritual significance of dreams, say that we must probe their depths for ourselves.

"That is the way it should be," she told me. "I tell every new student to read the twelfth chapter of the book of Numbers, particularly, the sixth verse: 'Hear now my words: If there be a prophet among you, I the lord will make myself known unto him in a vision--,' "this three-dimensional world of ours is the place of vision," she interjected, '--and will speak to him in a dream.'"

"Doesn't that mean," I said, "that we have to rely on you and others like you who purport to understand dreams to interpret them?"

"No," she countered, "by a 'prophet,' this verse doesn't mean 'a' person among persons with this gift, but a faculty that can be roused within yourself, because it's there. It can be roused, if you desire it strongly enough. You have to think of the *Bible* as a monologue staged as a dialogue."

"What authority do you have for that?" I asked.

She smiled indulgently. "Oh, how the world loves to lean on what it recognizes as authority!" she said. "If you have degrees hooked onto your name, that makes you someone who should be listened to, and the news media fall all over themselves to report what you have to say. I have no degrees, so I don't ask anyone to lean on me, as person, for authority. I say that the understanding of your dreams is a gift that is latent within you. Just as Numbers says. A good many of my students accept the idea that our *Bible* should be read as a monologue. Some of them interpret their dreams beautifully.

"You don't think it's a monologue staged as dialogues? God talking to Himself? Go back to the time our Gospels came into existence, and to the time of the neo-Platonists of Alexandria. They put forth the idea that all the world's scriptures should be studied as events that take place within spiritually awakening Man. One of them, Philo Judaeus, perceived that two different levels of experience were being communicated in all sacred writings. Is that good enough authority?"

"I'll accept it.

"If you want a modern reference, you might have a look at *The Metaphysical Bible Dictionary* put out by the Unity School of Christianity. It's filled with the same idea, that your being and God's being is one and the same. Therefore, all dreams are God's dreams about Himself, even if I don't use that word, 'God,' often."

"I've noticed."

"I usually say 'Consciousness.' Nobody argues with that. It doesn't offend anybody. But the two are synonymous."

"And if I accept that?"

"Then your dreams will give evidence of it."

"In what way?"

"Years ago a newspaper writer, Jim Bishop, wrote a column called, 'Jesus Christ Comes to Call.' It was about a man who was disturbed by the state of the world. In response to his prayer, 'Send Jesus Christ down here,' a voice within him said, 'You are Jesus Christ.'"

"That's interesting. Who was the man?"

"I don't know. But that's what I mean. What I said about getting evidence of your divinity from within. From your inner Self."

I started to say more but Vivian broke in, "The man that Bishop wrote about mistakenly took the message to mean that he, himself, was the historical Jesus come to earth again. He went out and tried to convince others of it. God had said so to him. He didn't get far. He didn't understand what he'd been told. Jesus Christ was not, and is not, one solitary man, then or now. He is equally within all. He is the only man who lives or ever will live."

Again I wanted to comment but she didn't want me to interrupt.

"How anyone interprets his dreams, or other inner activity, such as this man's response to this prayer, is dependent on his consciousness of himself. God is asleep, dreaming that He is Man, awake. All this is His dream," she said gesturing toward the outside world, "and He is the only One who wakes.

When He does wake, you know that you, are He. If you see dreams as I do, they are a communication from the depth to the surface. From the Soul of the universe, God--Consciousness--to what It currently understands of Itself, identified as the person you know by your name."

"This lifts dreams from the mundane to the sacred," I said.

"Any other stand reduces the sacred to the mundane," she replied. "That's why I feel the study and discussion of dreams should be the province of the churches. If you could get them to accept the unitary nature of being, which many don't. They are wedded to a literal interpretation of Scripture, preaching 'Jesus' as an historical character, who as God incarnate, came in the flesh once and only once."

"Since, as a rule, churches don't discuss their members' dreams, how about the family circle?" I suggested.

"An excellent idea," she said. "It would be an interesting project for sociologists to set in motion. It's an area of collective behavior I don't think has been tried in our culture, although it has been practiced elsewhere."

"There's a tribe of people--the Temiars--on the Malay peninsula," I said.

"I was thinking of them. I know a little of their dream practices," she said. "At breakfast, parents discuss their night dreams with their children. Then the children's dreams are discussed. Later, in tribal councils held by the elders, the process is repeated, the parents' dreams and the children's dreams come in for yet more examination and discussion. These people have one of the most emotionally mature societies on earth. In comparison with so-called civilized societies, they have almost no crime."

"Are you saying that the attention they give to their dreams is responsible for this?" I asked.

"No, that would be too simple. They are a small, closed society with little mobility. Then there's the matter of racial homogeneity. They have some crime but not on the scale we do. We're heterogeneous. We have great mobility, plus other factors. The thing about the Temiars is that their interest in the dreams of their children puts them on a par with the adults. They have equal status and they know it. Consequently, they are integrated into their society at an early age, and more smoothly, because of equal footing with their parents before their elders in the respect paid to their dreams."

"How could we go about imitating this?" I asked. "Any ideas? It would seem to have some beneficial effect on building family solidarity, if nothing more."

"You've got me. I don't know. Except for maybe some of the more liberal churches taking up the initiative in setting up dream councils. They might try to get their people to handle dream discussions in the family, then bring them into the councils with the children for group discussion.

"That's one thought," she said, "but with our hang-ups, dreams being given little respect--in bad repute, really, I don't have an answer. Except more education. More interest in dreams. More attention to their spiritual significance. A serious concern with the Biblical dictum that all dreams come from God. Maybe, if more attention to the value of our dreams was given to newspaper and magazine readers--such as articles about the Temiars--families would take it up on their own without waiting for the clergy to prod them into it."

"If you had the chance to say something on the subject to people of diverse religious faiths, what would you say that might cut across all the dividing lines of the numerous creeds and sects in this country?" I wanted to know. "Is there a common denominator, something they might all agree to?"

"One thing I might say," she said. "I'd remind them that Jesus always taught in parables. Whoever you are, your dreams are your 'Jesus' speaking in parables to you."

Chapter 15

LIFE IS LIKE UNTO A DREAM

Vivian and I had been discussing how to get American families to discuss their dreams with one another, for better family solidarity, as members of some primitive societies do. It is of worth in helping to produce emotional maturity in the young, as the practice of the Temiar people on the Maley peninsula has proven.

"They have a common agreement on what their dreams mean to them." she said. "They are animists and see spirits in everything: in trees, in rocks, in waterfalls. How they interpret their dreams, I don't know, but within the context of their psychology it works well for them. If some accord in our society could be reached on the nature and the meaning of dreams, it would create a base for discussion. I don't know if that can be achieved. We are diverse in our views. And biased in them."

"If you could lay some base for it, what would you want to go into it?" I asked.

"That's easy for me," she said, "because dreams are totally spiritual. They come from and deal with ultimate reality. But if I raised that in a group of any size, there would follow a dozen arguments on the meaning of ultimate reality.

"So to cut across as many lines as possible, I think I'd lay it down like this to forestall argument: for all of its seeming solidity, know you not that this life, verily, is like unto a dream?

"The intensity with which Consciousness is focused in any state produces what we describe as the reality of that state. In my work as a dream interpreter, I've had people tell me with conviction that they have been 'awake' in their dreams. The walls of buildings, the keystone arches of railway stations, the bottles and jars lining drugstore shelves, the touch of cash register keys, are as solidly real, apparently, in their dream states as they are in this world around us.

"I cannot prove or refute their statements but I can accept the possibility of their experience just as I can believe a person under hypnosis can see things he is told to see, describe foods he is told to taste, and taste those foods, although no food is present to the senses.

"There are differences, and similarities, between our dream experiences and our life experiences. But the similarities are greater than the differences. Perhaps the chief difference between the two states is the sense of continuity we enjoy in this terrestrial world. Unless someone moves us from our beds during the night to another location, we wake where we were before we laid down to sleep. We see the same bedroom walls, the same bedcovers.

"The world of dreams is more fluid, more dynamic, than this solidly real three-dimensional world in which we spend two-thirds of our lives. In dreams we are not bound to physical limits. The dreaming faculty that I call The Dreamer, freed from Its focus in physicality, ranges widely in Its fantasizing productive power. It synthesizes experiences we could not conjure in the waking state. Nonetheless, no matter how bizarre our dream experiences may be, they correlate with life in that our dream figures move in time and space. Our dream people act, think, and feel in ways that are familiar to us. True, the time that elapses during a dream that lasts but a few minutes to some researcher studying the eye movements of a dreaming person, may portray events lasting several hours. Every world, whether that of dreams or that of our twenty-four hour day, has its own reality and who is to say which is the more real? Consciousness is all that gives reality to anything and there is no device beyond Consciousness with which to measure this or any other world.

"Turn on your television set and perhaps you will see a program where people are sitting in a parlor conversing and enjoying coffee. Turn to another channel and you may see a man boarding an ocean liner. Then you see him debark. A car picks him up and speeds him to an airport. He gets on an airplane and the plane takes off. Turn back to the first program and the parlor crowd has scarcely yet tasted its coffee. You, as the television viewer, have a different sense of time than do the actors in the separate programs. Each has his own sense of space-time reality. Only because you know they are electronic pictures seen objectively as flat patterns on a screen do you say they are unreal. Your entry into either scene, subjectively, to play a part in the lives of the others, would make it real for you.

"Both television programs had the same locale for you, the observer of them. When you switched from one channel to another, you didn't see the second program at a different place in your room, or outside your window on the lawn. This world of ours is fabulous for it contains worlds within worlds, each with its own distinct sense of space-time reality, not removed from the others, that interpenetrate each other without interference. You don't move from your bed at night, yet you enter an entirely different world. All you need to shift from one to another is a change of consciousness.

"In my opinion, this world of ours, so dense and difficult, is a field for the gaining of experience that can be gained in no other way. All the horror, the pain, the cruelty that takes place between the characters is certainly real while it lasts, but it is only a tempor-reality from a loftier sense of being than what we know in our present identification. An intimation of this is in Isaiah, the fifty-first chapter. It says to look to the heavens, the earth beneath. It will all vanish like smoke, wax old like a garment. All who dwell therein shall likewise die. The text declares at the same time, 'My salvation shall be forever,' meaning, I feel, that the One Being who authored it, Consciousness, rouses Itself, wakes, and extracts Itself from all these identifications."

She touched my sleeve, then her own, at the words, continuing, "There is a Dreamer dreaming us. But, more precisely, each is that Dreamer, having suspended a superior consciousness to enter into the life of this 'Three-D' dream, I call it, for educative purposes. Like unto our rising in the morning from

112

our nightly dreams, so Consciousness emerges from this life, taking with It that which It could not know without having become Its dream figures."

"This is hard to embrace," I said.

"I know. Our world seems so indestructible. So permanent. Yet the hardiest, longest-lived organisms on the face of the globe have but a brief duration. They are all just as transient as smoke. The bristlecone pine is over four-thousand-years old, still living, still growing, but it, too, is doomed."

"Where does reality leave off and unreality begin?" I asked.

"There is no unreality to awakened Consciousness. All is contained within It. So there can be nothing extraneous to That Which Is: Consciousness. For that would imply an impossible form of Is-ness."

"How do I know this?"

"You have to 'wake' to it. While you are in it, this world is your sole reality, just as your night dream constitutes your sole reality when you enter that world. The dream world is a world within your world from which you would never escape, if you never woke from your dream. It would constitute the totality of your life, wouldn't it?"

"I guess it would."

"You know eventually your night dream ends and you emerge from it. Just as the dream ends with the dawning day, so your life dream will end sometime. Until it does, That Which Is Conscious-- capitalize those words," she requested, "--conscious of existing as the person by whose name you call yourself, goes right on living and experiencing with no break in continuity, no loss of identity.

113

"At the time that others call your 'death,' you find yourself in a world like the one in which you now find yourself, for it's this world of living, breathing men that must be encountered and endured until all possible conceivable states have been experienced."

"And when they have been experienced?"

"Then you 'wake.'"

"Just like that?"

She nodded. "But not until 'Christ' be formed in you--as you--according to the *Bible*, does the 'life dream' end. At that culminating event, you are 'resurrected,' and no longer enter the world of three-dimensions as 'one' among a multiplicity of persons.

"That's what has happened to me. I'm here for however long I yet may be in this 'garment,'" she touched her body, "only to tell my story, that others, having heard, may take heart and believe---and, having heard and believed, may, too, embody the experience.

"Or, as I sometimes do, I summarize it in verse:

> *Now I lay me down to sleep,*
> *I pray the Lord my soul to keep;*
> *If I should die, before I "wake,"*
> *Again, a role, I'm bound to take;*
> *But, if I "wake," before I die,*
> *My Consciousness I place on high."*

Chapter 16

AWAKE, O SLEEPER!

Vivian and I talked at length on the subject of life being like unto a dream, with some interesting conclusions: just as we wake to our daily world when our dreams of the night are over, so we wake to a higher reality when this life "dream" is over. It is an individual process: God, or Consciousness, realizing Itself where It has assumed the life of your person, and dwelt as that.

"All of us are conscious," she said, "but some of us are divinely Self-conscious."

"That must be anguishing to someone who senses it, but has not yet realized it."

"Yes, it is. The paradox of being human is one of both anguish and exaltation. Anguish, because we feel we cannot ever reach absolute perfection. Exaltation, because under no other conditions could we have any anguish whatsoever. The *Bible* equates our condition--this world--with a world of 'death.' 'Awake, O Sleeper, and rise from the dead.' We are given this admonition many times in scripture.

"To whom is it addressed? To physical bodies in graves? They have no ears. They hear nothing. Then those who do hear must be those referred to as dead. Dead to what? Dead to the sense of their own divinity. To whom could the words, 'Awake,

O Sleeper,' be addressed other than to That which entered into life with you, as you--Consciousness-- your awareness of being?

"It's been said that Man, God, and the universe are but different aspects of the same being. With only one source, all things are essentially That. Or here's how I've put it in one of my verses:

Everything's the same as me,
For all the differences that I see;
I project the sea of space,
My 'I' makes up the human race;
I travel faster than the eye can blink,
I'm present with the thought I think;
All is One, and One is free,
Another puts an end to Me.

"Capitalize the 'Me,'" she said, "it stands for Causation. Cause hides Itself in the grand playground of life, and Its multiplicity we see manifested as this universe, but it can never be separate from effect. The two are inseparable. Neither can exist without the other. There is no such thing as a one-ended stick, or a one-sided coin. Consequently, there being no otherness than 'cause-effect' joined, there can be no other than the One so joining."

"It isn't easy to adopt that sense of self, of being 'one' with the One," I ventured, "just by reasoning."

"No. It has to be experienced to be known. That's why life is pure grace, Divine grace, for the knowing comes to all, eventually. Until then, few of us are likely to realize how fragile is the foundation upon which we have built ourselves, how much of ourselves lies within the narrow range of our ideas and opinions and convictions that have grown from them. Our sense of self is based to some extent on these ideas and opinions. If so, its structure is so weak and tenuous that, in comparison, a cobweb has the strength of Gibraltar. This realization strikes sometimes with stunning impact, if we are brave enough to accept it, at those times when we find our cherished opinions threatened, our ideas under attack. The rush of blind, unreasoning reaction to what, apparently, threatens us should be a signal to us, rather than the screen it most often is, hiding our insights from us.

"When we get defensive in the face of opposition to our convictions, we should ask ourselves, 'Is our sense of self only in these ideas and opinions?' Then we have little substance, and perhaps our defense mechanisms are thoroughly justified in attempting to preserve what little substance we have.

"But with a better self-knowing comes a magnificent release from all the tension that held us like a coiled spring, ready to loose itself upon any provocation against those who challenge our precious attitudes."

"By self-knowing," I said, "you mean the higher sense of Self, the capital 'S,' Self?"

"Of course. Self-knowing is a vast vestibule through which the spiritual sense of Self is reached. The personal self must, at some time, be surrendered for this higher Self. The antagonism of the world has a salutary effect when it propels us in that one direction."

"We cling tenaciously to the personal sense," I said.

"It's all we know to begin with," she returned. "Our patterns of response are laid down early and the personal sense grows around them. They are difficult to uncover. They are difficult to surmount. Like grooves in a record, the needle wears the groove deeper when a situation arises to put us on the same old turntable, back in the old grooves. We remember and repeat what we have learned even though we can't recall the incidents that cut the initial tracks."

"Then we often come to value as truths what may not be truths at all," I supplied.

"Right. Beliefs shape our attitudes. We cling to them. We find our identity in them. When our foundation is in them, we know no other identity."

"Our convictions become our identities?"

She agreed. "They can. We can detect this in ourselves, if we can catch ourselves overreacting in the face of opposition to our pet ideas."

"Our ideas and convictions are not always wrong."

"No. But when we get fearful, angry, or belligerent it can be a clue that maybe our identity is built on them. Identity is precious, if it's the right identity--a true, imperishable sense of Self, an identity not built on the accumulation of ideas and opinions about ourselves. Honest self-appraisal and self-knowing are indispensable requirements to finding that identity."

"But it's possible," I said, "that the identities of those who challenge us may be no deeper than their convictions either."

"True! That's what makes it such an interesting game. Not leaning over backwards to accept others' opinions, and not too readily throwing away our own, requires much in the way of discrimination and testing. To grow a new sense of Self isn't easy, but nothing worth having comes easily. We must want it enough to tear away all the scaffolding built up around our persona, not clinging to it, or reinforcing it. To turn around in our thinking, to pursue metanoia, is like demolishing a building. Until the old structure is torn down and removed, a new one can't go up on the same site.

"Each of us is a house with many rooms. There are dark rooms in it. Some rooms have locked doors. Doors that squeak on their hinges--they haven't been opened for so long. There are rooms holding secrets that we don't want anyone to know about. Rooms whose walls are lined with pictures of ourselves we think bright and beautiful. But pictures whose glass is cracked, whose frames are twisted, whose portraits are faded and mildewed, if we can stand them in the light.

"The contents of this internal house of ours are shown to us in our dreams. In the daytime, too. But we notice it mostly in dreams because there's nothing veiling it. Persona is stripped off while we sleep. When Consciousness stirs where It has lain buried, and begins to rouse Itself from Its long sleep, we see what sort of dwelling place we've been, what kind of place we have provided for It. We get an

119

inventory of our habitation from cellar to attic. We get glimpses into the silent housecleaning process. We see whether we're helping, or hindering, and how far the job has progressed.

"We have to be able to withstand the unpleasant truths about ourselves that dreams portray. A dream doesn't care what it says. Or to whom. About anyone. A dream says it like it is. Always. Dreams are searingly truthful. But their purpose is benign. To show us to ourselves as we really are. To help us grow toward integration and wholeness.

"It takes shocks to awaken, and our daily life and our dreams give them to us a-plenty when the time comes for Consciousness to 'awake.' In the twenty-fourth chapter of Matthew, Jesus is shown the buildings of the temple by his disciples. The temple is Consciousness. We are the buildings. And He says, 'Verily, I say unto you, there shall not be left one stone upon another, that shall not be thrown down.' To me, that's our own inner structure built up in life from literal thinking. All of it has to go. But all of it. In dreams we can see the furniture gone from our house. That's usually a good sign. Or the insides may be gutted from top to bottom. Another good sign. It shows the work of inner regeneration has begun.

"There can be dozens of things besides seeing one's house emptied that convey similar meaning. Earthquakes in dreams are a good example, with buildings crumbling. Or elevators filled with many people that go crashing down. Wrecks of all kinds employing your personal belongings. Your car, for example. That's a common one. Or your clothes can be in tatters. That's always good for a shock, to feel your best suit ripped to pieces and made useless. These are almost sure indicators that the work of removing <u>persona</u> has begun. When people have these dreams they often wake in panic at what's happening. Why not? These experiences can be devastating, but the awakening can't be prevented. It can only be delayed, or accelerated, but it can't be put off forever. So why delay it?

"We can draw back from awakening, or we can yearn for it and embrace it. To be small in our human condition, or to invest it with grandeur, is one of the important choices we are offered. If we're bound to the personal sense of self, the awakening can be unnerving. Life is unnerving, too, if we choose to shrink ourselves by marinating in our woes, seeing the world as hostile, and ourselves as abandoned to a dismal, isolated fate. In such case, the edge of darkness on which we live can engulf us, and we can lose that little consciousness we have snatched from that dark, unknown continent of amorphous being. We can surrender what has been previously gained and return to that void from which Mankind, as a race of semi-civilized creatures, has so recently emerged.

"It is difficult to be Divinely conscious, with all the danger and daring it implies. But in the end, it is the only choice. The other alternative is oblivion. The Scriptures say, 'Choose ye this day whom ye will serve. . . he who finds me, finds life. . . he who misses me, injures himself. . . he who hates me, loves death.'"

Chapter 17

TO INTERPRET A DREAM, BE AWAKE

Some of the early arrivers at Vivian's dream sessions one bright summer morning were questioning her about her pet subject: "Interpret Your Daily Life as You Do a Dream," with reference to the problem of good and evil.

There were not many present at the moment. Just a few ladies. Outside, through a large picture window bracing each side of a red, brick fireplace, a young squirrel scampered along a retaining wall. A California blue jay scolded him from an overhanging limb of a live-oak tree. The squirrel stopped, looked up, and chattered back at the jay.

"The jay would like to find the squirrel's nuts," Vivian observed, "and the squirrel would like to have the eggs in the jay's nest. They're both mischief makers, but, of course, they don't see it that way. The mischief in the other is in each one of them, just like the mischief we see in another is in ourselves. But we're blind to that. No one does deliberate evil from his viewpoint. The bank robber is doing good for himself. So is the kidnapper, the extortioner, or any other law breaker.

"Which reminds me of an incident that took place on a street corner in San Francisco," she continued. "A film crew was shooting a scene from a new version of <u>Dracula</u>, called 'Blackula,' the starring role being played by a black man. He wore a black, hooded cape, a black skull cap, and he had a couple of long, fang-like, white teeth. A little old lady who had been observing what was going on between scenes, came up to him and said, 'Are you the villain?' Somewhat surprised, he drew himself up and replied, 'Well, I don't think so!'"

That brought a laugh from everyone in the room.

By this time others were arriving, helping themselves to coffee in the kitchen, and joining the discussion group. One of them asked her to talk about the 13th verse of the Book of Habakkuk in the Old Testament. I turned to it and read it to myself in order to stay abreast of the discussion:

> *Thou are of purer eyes than to behold evil, and canst not look on iniquity: wherefore lookest thou upon them that deal treacherously, and holdest thy tongue when the wicked devoureth the man that is more righteous than he?*

As I listened to what the members of the group were saying, I reflected that evil has always been a great theological problem. Present day Christians and Jews are as much disturbed by it as have been philosophers and thinkers down through the ages. Men believe that evil is an unchanging fact of existence, yet few can abide it.

"The writer in Habakkuk reflects in the 13th verse that state of Consciousness of one who is lost in the world of opposites, identified as one of the characters in the drama, questioning why the Lord refuses to take the part of the good man as against the wicked one. The devout church goer asks the same question: 'If God is Love, why does He permit evil?' To me, the explanation is simple. If you don't want a world of shadows, you have to settle for one without light. Take your choice. You can't have one without the other," Vivian expounded.

The group was silent.

"'I form the light, and create darkness; I make peace, and create evil: I the Lord do all these things,'" she said, quoting Scripture. "Read it in Isaiah. Everything going on around us in the visible world, no matter what you name it, is the play of Consciousness in duality. It is a grand, dream play, like a stage play, for you don't see the producer directly. You only see him by the actions of the characters. So, I say, to interpret a dream, you have to be 'awake.' You have to, in a sense, come off stage. You can't see that a dream is a dream while you are convinced you are one of those in it, can you? You have to come out of it, at least part way, before you can do that. You come out of the night dream when you come off your bed. But you come out of this three-dimensional dream of the day, by positioning yourself as The Dreamer. Mentally, you put your own little character down on stage with all the others. The way to exercise control over your responses to the 'Three-D' dream is to be so thoroughly in charge of yourself as The Dreamer that you don't fall into states unwittingly. When you see the 'devourer' taking advantage of the 'righteous,' as Habakkuk says, you, as Consciousness observing the play, don't enter into blind reaction and get caught in it because you see both sides as states--"

"You're too pure to hold either 'good' or 'evil' as realities in themselves," interjected the one who had brought up the subject.

"That's it!" Vivian responded enthusiastically. "One state seems better than the other, but keep in mind they illustrate the bipolar activity of Consciousness. The activity is not The Actor. You, Consciousness, are the One who acts. Forgetful of that, you fall into opposites and are played by them. You lose your dominion as The Dreamer and become like unto one of the dreamt."

There were moments of silence as we considered what she had said. I glanced out the window. The squirrel had disappeared from the retaining wall. The blue jay had flown from the branch.

"If you really know that you are Consciousness," she added, "you know that both 'good' and 'evil' are only illustrated concepts. Then you are of 'purer eyes' than to take sides with either."

"If they are only concepts," came a voice across the room, "then who, or what, is the 'devil'?"

"That question is very often asked here," she replied. "The word, 'devil,' is 'lived' in reverse. Spell it backwards--'l-i-v-e-d,' that's the devil. Doesn't life bedevil us when we live it in reverse--unaware that the Conscious Awareness of Being is the author of it all?"

What she had just said amused her and she laughed saying, "If we really were aware of it, we couldn't live in reverse!"

She paused, then said, "Let's go back to the Book of Job. We are shown Satan parading before the Lord. The Lord says, 'Where did you come from?' Satan answers, 'From going to and fro in the earth, from walking up and down in it.'

"Okay, there's your opposites. The 'to' and the 'fro.' Being either attracted to, or repelled by what you see or encounter. Habakkuk says something about that, too. Read beyond the 13th verse of the first chapter. It says that men are made 'as the fishes of the sea.' They have no ruler over them. A fly may fall onto the surface of the water and a fish is attracted to it. Stir the water with a stick when the fish approaches and it darts away. We're no better than fishes, most of us. We are taken up 'with the angle.' We are hooked. Caught in the net. Gathered into the drag, when we haven't discovered our true identity, as Consciousness, and live accordingly. Look up Habakkuk's words. He finishes by saying that men who make their living from the sea offer incense and sacrifice to Heaven in thankfulness for providing them with creatures so stupid as fish."

"But you certainly can't ignore evil," someone broke in.

"No," she agreed, "you can't ignore it. It says in the twelfth verse, just preceding the one we've been talking about, that it's given to you--"

"For judgments and corrections," someone said in anticipation.

"Yes." Vivian opened a *Bible* to the Book of Habakkuk and read the twelfth verse, "--thou hast ordained them for judgment; and, O mighty God, thou hast established them for correction.'"

"For discrimination and evaluation?"

Vivian acknowledged the question with a nod. "It's all played out for Consciousness' sake. You bring everything back to Cause by seeing what aspect of Consciousness can function in the manner that is being made visible to you. The reason for conflict in the world is that we think we have the right to use force against others. On the first three levels of interpreting, man acts like this: at the physical, instinctive level he calls what he senses, to be either pain or pleasure. At the mental level, he calls it right or wrong and looks for something to blame. At the moral level, he calls it good or evil and tries to straighten out the subject he thinks is to blame. We try to right wrongs by force and violence instead of assigning it to Consciousness. 'Vengeance is mine,' sayeth the Lord, 'I will repay.' But how many of us are content with that? No, we run for lawyers and start lawsuits. Or we call in the government."

"Yes, but what do you do if you're put upon by others?"

"What do I do? I see it for what it is: domination. A distortion of freedom. What has true freedom and dominion? Consciousness. Consciousness has dominion over everything. If I'm convinced that Consciousness is what I am--really convinced--I can't live under domination, at least not for long."

"It sounds simple."

"Simple but not easy," Vivian replied. "I never tell anyone it's easy. It's the hardest thing in the world, coming away from that first sense of self as a person among persons, doing that <u>metanoia</u>, that

128

radical turn around as to who and what you truly are. You will fall back into reaction, instead of reconciling a state in Consciousness, many times. That's why I like so well that particular Beatitude, 'Blessed are they that mourn for they shall be comforted.' What does that mean, not literally, but on the spiritual level? I take it to mean that when you backslide and go into a state of reaction and behave as one of the dreamt, you mourn over it. You truly do. I do. By the same token, the comforting comes in the mourning for it shows that when you recognize you know what you've done. The next time, it should be a little easier to keep from slipping into a state and being captured by it. I tell students, 'You must watch from moment to moment.' It demands vigilance. It's rugged work, and I'm the first to admit it. When it comes to doing this work, you'll go into despair many times when you discover how weak and frail you are."

Chapter 18

TO INTERPRET A DREAM, BE AWAKE

The room was filling with people and Vivian took some time to brief them on the subject under discussion.

"If the Tree of Good and Evil was to materialize in front of us now, and everyone was given a knife and asked to cut off what is evil, it would shortly be reduced to a stump. It would be as Thoreau said, 'Thousands hacking at the branches of evil for one who is striking at the root.' What I might leave on the tree as good to me, someone else might cut off as evil. What I in turn might cut off as evil, he might leave as good, if it were possible to take a knife and separate the two. But it isn't. It would all grow back again because you can't separate them. They are part of the eternal nature of things. So leave that tree alone. I say in one of my spiritual jingles, 'The bad about good is it won't last. The good about bad, it, too, shall pass. That Tree is a snare, illusion its root. False are the branches, producing its fruit. Called "Good-and-Evil," that Tree, of the fall. Borrows its life, then perishes all.'

"But you don't perish. Not if you don't eat of it. In Genesis we're told to eat of the Tree of Life, to shun the Tree of the Knowledge of Good and Evil. Everything on it is mixed fruit. You can't help

131

tasting the opposites no matter what you bite into. Sweet and sour come together. So what do you do about that 'tree'? You strike at the root. Not literally, but by seeing what it is in which all phenomena are rooted: Consciousness. What you see on that tree are illustrations of Its dreaming Self, and if you grant credence to illustrations, you are apt to get caught by them.

"Everyone would like to acquire riches and escape poverty. But anything pursued in one direction too long becomes its own opposite when it passes the meridian point. Night turns into day, day into night. Did you ever know a man who lost his health acquiring riches? All his money will not buy his health back so he's poorer than the man who has health. When the stomach is filled, hunger turns to satiety. A second helping tastes fine, but a third produces a stomach ache. Pleasure turns into pain. This drama of life wouldn't be, if it wasn't for opposites. You can't have heroes without villains. Cops without robbers. Persecutors without scapegoats. 'It's the ardor of the assailant that makes the vigor of the defendant,' Emerson said. True. Look at America's Watergate. As a nation, it was an anguishing experience. Some sided with the President. Some sided against him, until, finally, the pressure became so great he resigned, the first American President in our history to do so. Did the Watergate burglars do evil? Not in their sight. Even the President didn't admit to wrongdoing when he left office. He said he'd made 'mistakes' but he thought they were in the best interest of the country. I'm not the judge of that, but it shows how we all are when we are identified with our roles."

Someone asked a question, "What are you getting at?"

To that she responded, "What I'm getting at is how to handle the problem of 'good' and 'evil'--see through both to their source. What is causing it? Watergate, to me, proves what I once read, that throughout man's history, it has been true, generally, that when evil grows insufferable it touches the point of cure. Everything we see around us is being played out at the will of One, ever present Identity. Don't you think that's a good play on the word, 'President'? I do!" she said, laughing. "Here's a dream that's relevant, illustrating it perfectly:

> *"I was in a banquet hall. On a table was a caricature of Richard Nixon. Next to it was a caricature of the caricature which the artist modified. While looking at the two of them, I picked up a black grease pencil and said to myself about the second caricature, "The artist didn't give him a firm enough jaw line." So I stroked in a good strong jaw line. A senator saw me and when I turned away, he looked around to see if anyone was watching and when there wasn't, he rubbed the line out. All this took place at a grand party in Washington, D.C. It was held in a sumptuous place and there were many people present who were not members of the government. Privately, each official had given himself a name unknown to the rest of the people present. Each had a false name. Mr. Nixon, too. The idea was that in event of a national crisis, that name for the President would*

be announced over a public address system to alert him without causing a general panic. Every important official had a false name by which he could be identified without alarming non-government guests. Then all of a sudden Mr. Nixon was in our midst, very disorderly, drawing attention to himself by his profanity, making a disturbance, like a drunken man, so that all eyes were on him. I picked him up under the left arm-pit, someone else picking him up under the right arm-pit, and we carried him out, screaming and cursing against our removing him from the room. We were no sooner outside than he jumped out of our arms. He then straightened his hair and his tie and he was sober. He walked back into the room through a different door, very dignified, as though the first Nixon had been an imposter. Now the real Nixon had arrived. Then I found myself seated with two other men on a stairway elevator, like those in private homes for elderly persons who cannot walk, to take them up and down. The stairway in this place was circular and it went up three floors to the top. We ascended swiftly, passing many well-dressed people walking up the spiral staircase to a large auditorium. That scene vanished and I found myself downstairs where I'd been before, on ground level. This time I was in a large, beautifully appointed barroom. The back bar had shelves lined with black velvet. Indirect lighting from beneath made the glassware glow with a silver-like color. It was expensive Steubenware glass: highball glasses, wine glasses, champagne glasses, every kind of glass imaginable for serving drinks. There were many bartenders behind the long bar dressed in *red cutaway coats. Crowds of people were enjoying this cocktail party. I saw Mr. Nixon again. There was a clear bottle on the bar that contained a colorless liquid, an extract of ginger. When I looked at Mr. Nixon, he was only three-feet tall. He took a drink from this bottle and when he did, he turned beet red and complained how hot this drink was."*

Vivian put down the account of the dream and said with amusement, "I just love that first part of it, the part about the caricatures. Notice the second caricature was altered by adding a line to the jaw which was then rubbed out by a senator. The 'jaw' is a symbol of strength for we often think of a person with a firm jaw as strong-willed, and a person with a weak jaw as weak-willed. Obviously, each of the participants in the dream scene preferred to see Mr. Nixon differently, just as in life. It reminds me of something Johnathan Swift wrote, 'Imaginary evils become real by indulging our reflections on them, as he who in a melancholy fancy sees something like a face on a wall, can by two or three touches with a lead pencil, make it look visible, by agreeing with what he fancified.'

"Man is a 'caricature' of God and his imaginings are caricatures of himself. It is the repetition of the drama of life. Nothing on this earth has authenticity of itself. It is all a grand representation of the One who presides: The President. Or, to make the play on the word, 'present I-dentity.'

"We try to make the likeness to which we attach ourselves stronger than it deserves to be, by adding a mark to the jaw line. But someone else is

135

bound to take the opposite view and try to reduce the image we strengthen to what he feels it should be. So he rubs out the line when he thinks no one is looking.

"The one who is, presumably, the President has to portray every state, whether it is one of disorderliness or dignity. Consciousness brings Itself down to the level of our vulgar conduct. To remove him, of course, would be in order at that point. But when he comes back in, although it looks like another, there is only one President--'present I-dentity'--performing both parts. On the surface, it looks like someone imitating the President in an obnoxious manner, because when he comes in with his hair combed and his tie straightened, smiling, dignified, and so forth, what went on behind the scenes wasn't observed by the crowd. The President and his staff of officials had false names to begin with. The names we attach to ourselves are false. They are pseudonyms. We do this to placate the masses within ourselves--our many 'I's' as the late Dr. Maurice Nicoll called them--that would be alarmed to be recognized for what they are, fabricated identities-- just as we are--unless identified as Consciousness.

"The ascension on the elevator is understandable at this point. When we've gone behind the scene to perceive how everything is put together for show, for appearances, we've extracted the meaning from the whole performance and the 'play is over.' The play complete, all three interpreting modes rise as the One who knows the meaning, taking the knowledge with Him.

"The last scene is the aftermath, the celebration cocktail party following the great performance of this cosmic drama. The attendants are dressed in red, the garment of love. They serve in that position. All are partaking of what is being offered over this long bar. No one is left out. Once again, here comes the 'present I-dentity' personified as Nixon. He drinks something clear and colorless from a transparent bottle, meaning there is nothing clouding the contents of that which Consciousness imbibed in Its dream. But it has the effect of turning the personification 'beet red.' It's as hot as ginger. The whole performance was 'gingered up' by action and reaction to the point where at the reduced level of the three-dimensional world--symbolized as him being 'three-feet tall'--it seems discomforting.

"And it is," she added as a postscript, "the world is a burning place for all of us when we are identified as dreamt characters. But, as the dream shows, you, as Consciousness, having seen through it, escape it all by rising out of it."

I went to the window and looked out. I hoped the squirrel and the blue jay would come back again.

Chapter 19

THE WORST EVIL OF ALL

I stood looking out the window at the live oak trees beyond the retaining wall. The discussion of Good and Evil continued. I heard a woman tell her dream of playing a game of chess with the Devil.

"I found myself with my family and friends in an old house," she said. "All of us were in danger and I knew that to save them I had to play chess with the Devil. He was handsome and fascinating as we sat down to play. He tried to distract me. First, he offered me a drink. Then some refreshments. He would like to have seduced me, too--a suggestion I found not unattractive--but I kept my attention on the game.

"I moved a lamp on a nearby table and saw the real, ugly countenance of the Devil in the table's surface. I knew that if he knew that I knew how he really looked, I would be in even more danger."

Those present reacted with amusement at her evaluation of the situation. When it subsided she went on with her narrative. "I moved my bishop on the chess board to the queen's 'two' square and that was 'checkmate.' I had won the game. At that, the Devil turned into a wolf. I pushed him into a stove and from the fire emerged a beautiful man."

Before offering an interpretation of the dream, Vivian prefaced it saying, "I'd like to impress on everybody that every dream is telling <u>one</u> story with inexhaustible variations: redemption through sacrifice. God becomes Man that Man may become God. Every dream is a monologue staged as a dramatic dialogue, or dialogues, depending on the number of characters drawn into the dream scene. Sometimes there may be crowds present, again, a solitary figure or two with little or no speech at all. Yet the dream message is consistently the same: evolution through involution.

"In this dream an 'old house' in which one finds 'family and friends' is a familiar habitation with the associations that are most dear to us, the worthy acquisitions of life. To save them we are required to pit our skill against the Prince of This World, the Devil, who personifies the epitome of evil and error and falsity. A 'chess game' is a game of skill. It is one of the few games where the element of chance is ruled out. We win or lose by our own actions. No adversary is so formidable to Consciousness, lost to Its sense of Self while identified as <u>persona</u> in this three-dimensional world. The glare of this world's enticements, signified by the lamp, casts a fascinating glow on the world's attractions. It demands a strong will, a firm resolution, not to yield to the world's seductions, and the subject in this dream has that strength. She moves the lamp and looks beneath that which seems so attractive on the surface. There she sees reality. Not in the objective world, but in the subjective appraisal of what she sees. To discover this secret increases her danger. To know both sides of a subject increases temptation as it misleads us into thinking we can surmount its great danger. Knowing the truth, she moves her 'bishop, a symbol of the Christ, to the 'queens "two" square,' and 'checkmates' her opponent, winning the game. The 'queen' is the most powerful figure on the chess board. She represents the ruler of all the states of duality, signified by the 'two' square. Moving the bishop to the spot adjoining the queen, signifies a neutralization of temporal power with spiritual power. At this culmination, the Devil is now seen as one of the most fearsome and ravening of animals, a 'wolf.' There is an ancient alchemical symbol of a wolf burning in an athanor, or furnace. In the 'fire' of this world's experience all of the raw, untamed energy of the psyche is transformed and emerges as the purified Soul, symbolized by a 'beautiful man.'"

The dream and its interpretation stirred considerable comment from those present, and Vivian enlarged on the purifying fire with another dream. "In this dream a man was on a ship the size of a freighter that was anchored to a dock. On shore, a lot of houses were being built. There was much activity all around. He was aware of the sky, almost obscure, with a haziness hard to explain, but there was a window in it through which he saw much activity. An electrical tower flew by, then a lot of debris. He was seeing a war in progress with a lot of rockets, missiles, and explosions. Then the houses on shore started to burn. There were only a few others beside his wife with him on the ship. There was no fear. But he felt they should pull anchor and head for sea to get away from the fire on shore, if it should spread toward them. They would be safe anchored off shore instead of to the dock.

"He said he knew exactly what to do and gave calm orders to those about him to accomplish an orderly move. He told one person to gather food that had the most value and the least bulk, like 'raisins.' The war was still going on and he could see its turmoil through the window in the sky. Then he awoke.

"Since Noah's Ark, a 'ship' has symbolized the Divine Identity, the Self, or the Soul, meaning the capacity of Consciousness to identify. Anchored at the 'dock' means at the shore. The 'sea' and the 'shore' represent the two poles of Consciousness here. In Scripture these two poles are often portrayed as 'two brothers,' starting with Cain and Abel. The two poles are Consciousness 'awake' to Its eternal Divinity, or 'asleep,' living life as one's personal sense of self.

"The construction of 'houses' on shore represents the many states Consciousness erects for Itself. It takes up residence in all the limited concepts of Itself. This is the activity of our three-dimensional world, the multiple ideas with which the capacity of the Soul enters by identifying Self as 'I am this, I am that,' and you name it. The 'haziness' of the 'sky' has reference to Genesis 2:6, 'But there went up a mist from the earth.' This is the obscurity of Consciousness when Its sense of Self is polarized at the contracted limit of Man--meaning all manifestation as we know it, the word 'Adam' in Hebrew meaning of a 'low degree.'

"The 'window in the sky' symbolizes the Soul's viewpoint. The activity of powerful weapons reveals an explosion taking place within the Soul. The 'war' signifies that the Divine sense of Self is obliterating the personal based sense of self and its constructions and values. You can find a Scriptural correlation in Mark 13:2, 'Seest thou these great buildings? There shall not be left one stone upon another that shall not be thrown down.'

"The theme of this dream is illustrated in the Old Testament story of Lot leaving Sodom and Gomorrah. The cities could not be destroyed until Lot and his family left for a new country. The 'few' aboard the ship, like Lot's immediate family, personify that which is rightfully one's own. The 'wife' is the emotional nature, the Soul, and the 'others' are the eternal capacities of Consciousness outlined in Genesis as the Seven Days of Creation. These are Mind, Principle, Spirit, Soul, Life, Truth, and Love; united with The Dreamer as them all.

"There is no 'fear' where Love is in action. The feeling of the subject is to 'pull anchor' and cast off. Yes, cast away all the ties that keep one fixed to the 'shore'. To 'head for sea' means to journey to another medium, 'water' symbolizing infinite Truth traversed by the intuition, a different medium for the discernment of meaning. Being 'safe' lies in being 'anchored off shore,' beyond and away from the sense-based meaning of life.

"That the subject said he knew 'exactly what to do and gave calm orders' means he recognizes the inner process of Self-reconstruction, a calm and orderly, saintly and heavenly activity. The instruction

143

to 'gather food that had the most value and the least bulk,' means to select the most valuable ideas, like 'raisins.' This is a marvelous symbol for the 'grape' is the fruit of the vineyard and the 'vineyard' is the Soul. The 'raisin' is the grape after the water is pressed out, leaving only the essence, the most condensed and rich spiritual 'food,' represented here by this literal food.

"The 'warfare' continues until the demolishing in the Soul is complete. The subject awakes in this telling experience just as his Divinity wakes out of the life dream of being a 'person' to discover he is The Dreamer--not the dreamt--when Consciousness restores Its Divinity to Itself."

The group was silent until someone said, "Is there any worse evil than war?"

Chapter 20

THE WORST EVIL OF ALL

"When you ask if there is any worse evil than war, you are drawing us right back to the mundane world," Vivian replied, "because in the dream I just told you, 'war' has a beneficial outcome."

"But not in this world because nobody wins in a war. All the destruction, the horror, the pain, and everything in its wake," I rebutted.

"You are right in an overall sense," she conceded, "but like everything else, sentiments are often divided. War is profitable to some."

"Anybody who condones war for his profit is a scoundrel, the enemy of humanity, and a villain of the first order!" I snapped.

"You can't have heroes without villains," she rejoined. "The one goes with the other. Both are extreme definitions the One Dreamer makes of Itself. As each of us focuses attention, we see only overt appearance. But this is a world of paired opposites. That which is not dominant is recessive. As day moves toward night, following upon noon, so night moves toward day, following upon midnight.

"Anything reaching a meridian tends to become its own opposite. We have an exercise to perform. We have to pair opposites, mentally and emotionally, then bring them to Consciousness, spiritually, by asking, 'Who is taking this impression? What does it signify?' We have to stand outside of what we see in our daily drama, yet include it in that which is beyond 'person,' but which encompasses all: Consciousness."

"What's that to do with war?"

"Everything. In Its Selfhood, Consciousness is not any definition It is making of Itself. But It does so, forgetting who and what It is. What It assumes, It becomes, antagonists and protagonists alike. Antagonism is a mild form of war. Like all wars, it is generated by the deep 'sleep' of Consciousness as humanity, unaware of Its identity while so closed-down."

As the discussion continued, an argument was brewing. The arguer got offended at something Vivian said, then calmed down. "I see my mistake," she apologized. "I'm trying to tell you how to teach."

"Each of us is equipped with a vessel he carries to the ocean," Vivian consoled, "but whether it's thimble-size, or big as a bucket, it must first be emptied out before it can be filled.

"Let's get our discussion back on the spiritual plane, shall we?" she invited. "The worst of all evils is believing that you know when you don't know. Your mind cannot take in one new thing--not even a thimbleful--if it is already filled. Unfortunately, that is how most of us are."

She turned from the one to whom she had been speaking and addressed all of us. "You don't believe that you are in a dream, right now, do you? But I tell you that you are! You think you are a 'person' who is 'awake.' Whereas, you are Divinity, 'asleep.' In that state, all possibilities are constantly played and replayed, war being one of them.

"We think we are already fully conscious. So we don't strive to get what we think we already have. Yet our dreams, if studied, show us just how conscious we are, and offer us choices, if we care to make them. Almost every dream, no matter how slight, reiterates itself as the play of One identity in duality.

"Take this short dream, for example. It's a woman's dream. She is a white woman married in life to a white man. In her dream she said, 'I was married to a black man! There was a large race track in front of our home and he said to me, "I love to gamble."' That's all there was to it. To me, it says a lot. Her marriage to a 'black' man means that she is 'one' with the Infinite Unknown. The 'race track' is the course of the human race in this three-dimensional drama. The 'black' man loves to gamble. It is a daring risk that Consciousness as the 'black' man takes in becoming and animating the universe. It is a great gamble for when He enters the race, He does not know who He is. He doesn't know how to find Himself again, until He has completed the race!

"Those of you who read Maurice Nicoll's writings--and there are many here who do--know what he says, 'We feel shocked that Man cannot 'do,' can not stop quarrels, and wars, and so forth. We are driven by life, by what happens. We have nothing internal with which to resist.'[5] What I am doing is to give instruction on how to obtain a different concept

---

[5] Ibid., Vol. III., pp. 1248-50.

of 'self.' You are not just another one of 'the dreamt.' You are The Dreamer of it all. To find a change in oneself is 'to do.' To 'do' in a life sense is to react mechanically. That doesn't change you. To 'do' is to change the action of life on you by inner work on your daily impressions. If you know who you really are--The Dreamer, not the dreamt--at some moment when life impressions would make you violent, ugly, or negative, then you are beginning to succeed at Dr. Nicoll's concept that 'humanity is an experiment in inner evolution.'

"While in a dream you can be shocked, or gladdened, by things that happen, for that is your seeming reality. Your focus is so strongly identified as one of the dream characters that you are calling the objects around you from the position of being one of the dream figures there. You are calling yourself 'subject' and the rest 'object.'

"When you wake up you discover that all of the dream was subjective. If you can remember that you are The Dreamer, not the dreamt, as the incoming impressions are striking you, you don't need to feel shocked or depressed. When you are shocked or depressed, you are caught by the dream. One thing none of us can do, successfully, we can't lie to ourselves. The depths of our Being is an echo chamber of our motivations, sincerity, and attitudes toward life and ourselves. As one who is subject to fits of depression said to me, 'In my dreams I heard a voice say, "Depression is a tantrum."' So you see how this sort of indulgence is regarded on the Spiritual level.

"I'd like to go back and change something slightly, if I may," she said, taking a break in her discourse. "Minutes ago, I said that the worst of all evils is 'believing that you know when you don't know.' That is right enough but such belief comes from not knowing who you are, or refusing to accept it.

"God's mercy is infinite. Being infinite, He can forgive everything. Everything but one thing, that is. Scripture names one unforgivable sin, the sin against the Holy Ghost. In my orthodox Sunday School classes, it was preached often enough but we were never told what it was. So we felt guilty, as I did, because I probably had committed it, having done all else that was wrong. But it was never explained. When it comes to sinning against the Holy Ghost, it is the simple fact of failing to claim your Divinity. If you don't claim it, how can you think, feel, act, and perform as it? So who kept you from it? That can't be forgiven because 'forgive' means to 'give for' the mistaken view of yourself.

"If you forgive yourself for your mistaken view, you forgive yourself for having identified as a physical, separate entity because no created thing could gather its energy and cut itself off from its source and live independently of It. That is the greatest blasphemy. It's like Mickey Mouse standing up and declaring he is independent of Walt Disney. Do you understand now what the unforgivable sin is?

"Everything is based on your sense of identity. If you're based as a separate entity, you're in competition with the whole vast physical world of 'otherness.' Feeling that way, the world becomes fearful and encroaching. Therefore, you say you have to look out for 'number one' in your sense of 'number one' as your 'person' and defend it--and connive and exploit. You serve personal motive which keeps you bound.

"It is no longer, 'Thou shalt have no other gods before me,' for it is impossible to have any other God than Consciousness when you recognize that the name of this which is doing the recognizing is 'I' and you can't get away from it. Even if you deny it, it is still 'I' making the denial. So you haven't escaped it. Or like someone I heard say, 'Well, I'm not good enough to be God.' It is still God making the declaration from the present definition, saying the definition isn't good enough. And that's accurate. But it's still 'I am' defining Itself as lesser than Itself that isn't good enough. No definition can. That's why it isn't earned. It's pure grace.

"In Galatians it is referred to as 'adoption'--to be adopted as the 'Son of God,' the presence of Consciousness--and we call it 'assumption.' Don't mistake that word for 'presumption' and its connotation of arrogance. It isn't arrogant to assume what is rightfully yours. In fact, we're told to do it. That's what Scripture recommends. That's the good news. I call it 'resumption' because you always were It.

"The many in The One and The One in the many are connected. There are examples all through nature. Look at a tree."

As she spoke, I looked at one of the live-oaks outside the window. I studied its gnarled, twisted branches. I tried to follow one branch all the way to its end from the trunk through the branch, through the twig, to the outermost tip. Then from the trunk I followed other limbs and branches and twigs, each ending in a tip.

"'I am the vine, ye are the branches,'" Vivian was saying. Standing right in front of me was a fourth-dimensional symbol, the oak tree.

"They are not separate," she continued, "for when you took the position as one of the twigs-- thinking it had independent life and volition apart from the root--that illusion gave you a sense of loss, the other twigs all seemingly separate. So trace your Identity back to the root and recognize It as your wholeness and your perfection. Then think, feel, and act from it, that is the task. God assumes Man and Man must resume God. It's great art and there's no one to blame, not even your 'self.'"

Chapter 21

A DREAM INTERPRETER IS BORN

"Dream interpretation is an ancient art," Vivian said. "The Greeks called dream interpreters, 'oneirologists,' but the art predates the Grecian culture by many centuries. If you recall the Biblical Story of Joseph, the Egyptian Pharaoh elevated him to the highest position in his government as a reward for interpreting correctly Pharaoh's dream.

"And it was a Russian--Tolstoy, I believe--who held that The Story of Joseph in the Book of Genesis is the finest example of story telling ever written. That takes in a lot of territory. Unlike much of today's television story telling, wherein twenty minutes of film spin by while we grope between commercials for a clue as to what the story is about, we are told in the first four verses of the thirty-seventh chapter of Genesis that it's a story of conflict between Jacob's son, Joseph, and the remainder of his brothers. They hated him because of their father's special love for Joseph whom he favored with a gift of a coat 'of many colors.' Their enmity toward him was intensified by Joseph's dream wherein he said he saw their sheaves of grain bow down to his sheaf. And again another dream wherein Joseph's father and mother, as well as his eleven brothers, made obeisance to him.

"Fiction mimics life. The difference between great fiction and mediocre fiction is in the degree to which the shadow conforms to the substance. And this difference lies in the depth of the author's insight into the nature of reality, and with what accuracy he recreates it through his imagined characters. Whether an author takes a point in time and interweaves characters of his own with some who may have lived during the period, or whether all of his characters are of his invention, is just not of crucial importance. So the Book of Genesis should not be studied with an historical search warrant in hand but as a book of psychology that's as relevant today as it was those thousands of years ago when it was first written. We have to extract from the Biblical stories the esoteric truth about ourselves, to see how the acts and experiences of the people in Scripture are descriptive of the journey of the Soul through what we call life.

"I knew a Christian mystic named 'Neville' who once said, 'There is no fiction.' Then to prove his point, he described Morgan Robertson's novel about a fabulous ship that sailed the Atlantic loaded with the rich and complacent. It was wrecked on a cold April night on an iceberg. Robertson's book was titled, *Futility*. Fourteen years later the British White Star Line launched a ship like that in the novel. It was supposed to be unsinkable. But on April 19, 1912, the actual ship came to the same end as the fictional ship. The net worth of her wealthy passengers was over two-hundred-and-fifty million dollars, most of whom died in the icy waters of the Atlantic.

Robertson's ship was the Titan. The White Star liner was the Titanic.[6]

"The Story of Joseph is the story of Everyman, for your life and my life are God's life in miniature. Innocence must enter into experience that Divinity may expand Its own Self-knowledge. It does this by the great act of Self-forgetfulness, entering 'death's door,' birth into life through human generation. God becomes as we are that we may become as He is, but not before we are 'sold into Egypt' as slaves to the world of this three-dimensional life and experience. Egypt symbolizes spiritual darkness. Joseph's brother's are those ignorant, vain, jealous and vengeful sides of ourselves that cannot comprehend the spiritually endowed son of Israel clothed in multicolored splendor whose dreams foretell their subordination to him.

"The chief point is that the script was written before the drama was entered and began to unfold. The outcome is assured despite the obscurity of our present perspective. The power to dream and comprehend the meaning of this dream in which we find ourselves is resident within us all. When we have been made to serve Pharaoh's captain and have been thrown into 'prison,' the meaning of dreams begins to be made clear to us. Our perspective enlarges. We distinguish between the sense-based man, our former sense of self, and the new man, the spiritual overseer, who administers all of Pharaoh's affairs in Egypt.

---

[6] Neville, *The Law and The Promise* [DeVorss & Company Publishers, P.O. Box 550, Marina del Rey, CA 90291]

"At the stage where we disdain our dreams, we are playing the part of the young, naive Joseph and his vengeful brothers. The interpretive, intuitive faculty is 'cast into the dark pit,' so to speak, and the drama of our seeming isolation, finding ourselves to be 'one among seeming many' in this world, holds hardened sway over us and we are subordinated to circumstances.

"Then a great 'famine' descends over Egypt. We experience an inner hunger for sustenance and satisfaction beyond what our literal, worldly pursuits can give us and it clamors for our attention. When Joseph's brothers acknowledge Joseph and make obeisance to him, Egypt and Israel are reconciled. They are no longer divided. Neither surmounts the other. They are joined as one. In the domain of the spirit we find that dominion we strove so hard to find in the domain of the flesh. At last we are wise enough to articulate the meaning of the whole adventure. In the echo of Joseph's words to his brothers, 'It was not you who sent me but God,' we proclaim that all of that unto which we were sent was but God's own sending of Himself. Our will was only a seeming will for it was God's will, fated so, while He lived by the assumption of being Man."

Her beautiful soliloquy produced a rapt attention from the assembly, broken at last by someone who asked, "Where did you get this interpretive ability?"

"Would you believe that back in the Sixties it was the most unlikely thing in my mind?" she responded. "At that time, in 1965 I had no interest in dreams. I was a business woman, although always on a search for a more meaningful purpose in being, in all my pursuits. One day a friend of my husband's, who was in the salvage business, gave him a box of books which he brought home. I sorted them and was attracted to a small, slim book with the title, *Freedom For All*.

"I began to read this book and found that the author was taking some of the stories found in the Old Testament on a psychological level. Reading it was like listening to fine music at a concert where every nerve in your body begins to tingle with it. I'd never had that sensation before in reading anything. Something was striking my emotions in a way they had never been touched before.

"I liked the author so much I wondered if he had written anything else, so I wrote to the publisher. Several weeks passed and one day I got a postcard in the mail from a book store in San Francisco by the name of Lord and Jordan. The card was an announcement that the author of my special book was to be a speaker in the city soon. His name was 'Neville.'

"I didn't make any connection immediately between my receipt of the announcement card and my previous inquiry to the publisher. And I had a difficult decision to make because I had a phobia about riding in automobiles as the result of a nearly fatal auto accident I had suffered several years earlier. I was living in Santa Clara, fifty miles from San Francisco. 'Am I going to die a coward's death--and take that Bayshore freeway for an hour to go hear this author?' I asked myself, 'or am I going to miss it because of my fear? Which is going to win out here?' I decided I was going to go, if I had a way to get there.

"I don't remember who took me but I went. And I was sitting near the front, close to a man who was making a tape recording of the speaker's subject, 'Imagining Creates Reality,' when at the close of the speech the stranger turned to me and said, 'Have you read Neville's book, *Prayer, the Art of Believing*?'

"I said, 'No, is it on the book table?' I had noticed a long table at the rear of the auditorium when I came in. It was covered with books that were on sale by Lord and Jordan.

"'It is out of print,' he replied. And I thought to myself, 'If it isn't available, why did you tell me that?' Then I reflected on what the speaker had just been saying for the past hour, 'Imagining Creates Reality,' and I thought, 'Why don't you apply what you've just heard? Put it to a practical test. Here is an occasion to do so.'

"So as I left the auditorium I went by the book table again and scrutinized it. Most of the books on the table were by the speaker. They all had the same jacket, a picture of a tree with a heart on it, an eye in the center of the heart. So I imagined, *Prayer, the Art of Believing*, in the same jacket, lying on that table. I went home and forgot the whole thing. I was busy with a booth I had rented at the Santa Clara Country fairground and I didn't get back to the city again until the following Sunday.

"When I walked in the auditorium door, someone at the book table beckoned to me--I didn't know the woman--and said, 'Are you the lady from Santa Clara?'

"'Yes,' I said.

"'I have something for you,' she said as she reached down for a paper bag. She handed it to me and said, 'This is for you.'

"The crowd was moving in and I was taking up space at the door so I said, 'Thank you,' and backed off. I sat down in a seat and pulled out of that sack, *Prayer, the Art of Believing*. To this day I do not know what chain of events was set in motion for her to appear there with that book that night and hand it to me. There was no charge. It was simply, 'Here is that book that is out of print.' 'Really?' I thought. 'Yes, I can't deny the evidence of this. I know what I did.' I remembered the man who had told me that the book was out of print, and my thinking, 'What did you tell me that for?' and deciding to put it to the test. But this was so easy! This was so sudden!

"So I decided to try it a little more. 'Why don't I get some more books by this author?' I thought, because I had just then heard of another of his books that was out of print. *Out of This World*, was the name of it."

Chapter 22

A DREAM INTERPRETER IS BORN

"One night while sitting in an easy chair in my home, in my imagination I went to my bookcase and pulled out all the titles then current by Neville. On my imaginary table I then stacked them up. I picked each one up in my imaginary hands, read the title, got up and placed it in the bookcase--until I came to the one I didn't have--and did the same with it. I felt it, I read the title, and I put it up there. And then dismissed it.

"Three months went by. Again I found myself in San Francisco to hear a lecturer on spiritual awakening who had been recommended by Neville. His name was Freedom Barry and he announced some special classes of his. But as it was then nearing the Christmas holiday season, I was too rushed to attend. After the holidays, I wrote to him and got a card back announcing another series he was offering.

"'I'm my own boss,' I said to myself, 'I can take off whatever days I want.' So with friends who were also interested, once again I found myself in San Francisco. Freedom held his classes in a small room with about 18 people present. After the first class, as one of the ladies was leaving she said to Mr. Barry, 'I have two of them. I want to give this one to somebody. But I want to give it to one who will appreciate it, not just anybody.'

"With that statement, I did something I would not ordinarily do. I intruded on a conversation that did not include me. This is rude and discourteous, but my reaction was almost like that of a post-hypnotic suggestion. I stood up and said, 'Is it a book by Neville?' I couldn't think of the title. She pulled something from her purse, handed it to Mr. Barry, and he, looking at her, not at me, said, 'It belongs to this lady.' I looked at it and found it was *Out of This World*, by Neville. The book had no jacket. It was an old book, but the one I had pictured in my imagination in my bookcase along with his other books.

"I couldn't have told you the title of the book before the incident at the door between Mr. Barry and the lady. So much time had elapsed in the interim, it slipped from my mind what I had done. My realization of this was scary. 'I wonder how many other things I am bringing into my experience,' I thought, 'because I don't remember what I did.' Neville had said on many occasions during his San Francisco lectures that we are continually reaping the harvest that has grown from numberless forgotten plantings, because we exercise our imagination most of the time, unwittingly, rather than wittingly.

"I certainly couldn't remember the title of that book. That told me something. 'What are we doing morning, noon, and night?' I recalled Neville had said, 'Watch your inner conversations for you are writing a script that you will later enact.' Yes, imagination will do that. But this causative power that we all exercise, is that its supreme purpose? The getting of more material things? These were some of the questions I asked myself, once I was confronted with the proof of what I had done. Isn't there a more sublime purpose? I had to go further.

"Neville had told his audiences that we all live by our assumptions and that our destiny is to fulfill the highest of all assumptions: to be 'Christ.' Recognizing the personification of Jesus to be 'I-am-ness,' I began to go to sleep at night in the mood that I am 'unconditioned Consciousness.' If the assumption is impressed to the point of unswerving conviction, it hardens into fact, as I was to discover.

"From then on, radical changes began to take place in my life and living. Neville came back to San Francisco and I bought a tape recorder and went to his lectures. I also attended more of Mr. Barry's classes on 'spiritual awakening.' I took a week off and rented a hotel room in the city. Mr. Barry's classes were in the evening. When they were over I returned to my room and wrote summary notes on what I had gotten from his instruction. One evening I took some of my notes with me, and before class began I said to Mr. Barry, 'I wrote a summary.' He looked over my notes and said with surprise, 'Why, that's what I'm going to talk about tonight!'

"'Then how come I wrote it last night?' I asked, puzzled.

"'It just shows where you are in this awakening process,' he replied.

"It was during this time when I was away from business affairs and all my mundane concerns--while pondering these things from Freedom Barry's classes, where I had no phone and no salesmen interfering--that one night, like a bolt from the blue, came this audible command: 'INTERPRET YOUR DAILY LIFE AS YOU DO A DREAM!' I argued this with myself because I wasn't one to dream much, or have recall of them. But I couldn't put it down. So I included an account of the incident in my nightly summary and took it to Freedom's next class.

"Some of his people overheard me talking about it with Mr. Barry, and a lady said, 'Oh, I had a dream and I'd like to tell it to you.' So she did. I felt neutral, not knowing anything about dreams and was indifferent to what she was saying while she told it.

"The woman lived in San Francisco. She was an artist and a poet and a good many other things.

"She said to Freedom, 'I heard a voice in my dream that told me to 'paint the coast of California with a bell.' That was it--" Vivian paused. "Come to think of it. I told you about it early in these conversations, didn't I?"

"Yes," I answered. "You said you told her that she had a 'mission.' It was to refurbish her mind and emotions with better thoughts and moods."

"You remember it perfectly. California being her home state is often called the Mission State."

"Because of the missions established by Father Junipero Serra," I qualified.

"That's right. And I told you that both 'paint' and 'bells' produce colorful tones."

"Yes, and you said that to you the human eye is a mind symbol. The ear a Soul symbol."

"That's because impressions of color produced by paint reach the mind through the eye, while the tones of a bell reach us through the ear. But let's not go through all of that again. I mentioned it at this point because her dream was the first dream I ever interpreted. My response was automatic. I told her what it meant to me without my thinking about it. It came out of me as automatically as if someone had said, 'What time is it?' and you looked at your watch and said, 'It's ten o'clock.'

"She told others there what I said about her dream, and Freedom told all those present who had dreams to give them to me. And that's how I became a dream interpreter. I have to say with the Apostle Paul, 'I didn't hear it from a man, I didn't read it in a book,' it came as a revelation. There is no other way to account for this faculty. It is just there. The character you know by my name is no different than any other on the face of this earth. But I feel it was given me for the purpose of helping to convince others that our reason for being here is to fulfill Scripture. Each of us is meant to be identified as the central figure of the New Testament, a discovery that each of us makes in his own time.

"When you hear it from someone who has had the experience of it, that is the 'first coming of Christ.' When it happens to you, that is the 'second coming of Christ.' He is present now, as you, and that is the great Christian 'mystery.' Life through Death--the death of Divinity to become the life of all Humanity--that is the real meaning of the 'death of Jesus on the Cross.' The 'Cross,'" she concluded, extending her arms horizontally from her shoulders, "is, as William Blake said, 'the human form divine.' That is the 'Cross' upon which Christ is crucified. And it is not a painful crucifixion; it is a joyful one, for through it, He raises us to the level of Himself."

Chapter 23

"THE WIZARD OF OZ"

AND THE DREAM FORMAT

Many of those at this morning meeting I attended had heard Vivian's story of how she became a dream interpreter. While they took a coffee break, she told it to some of the new people, several of whom were youngsters.

"I had an interesting dream told to me by a girl not much older than some of you," she said. "This girl had been to the Middle East a couple of times. Prior to that, she had been involved in some of the political activism on the Berkeley campus during the latter part of the '60s. Here is what she dreamt:

"I found myself in the Far East, somewhere in India. I had just been arrested for the possession of 'grass.' I only had a little of it, but it made no difference to the powers there. It was a crime and they sentenced me to death by hanging. I was panic-stricken. I wanted to speak to my father for I was sure he could help me. He appeared and I told him what they meant to do to me. He shook his head sadly saying, 'Eventually, everyone must die.' I hoped my mother would save me and she appeared. When I told her my plight she also shook her head. My fear

mounted. My best friend appeared and fed me huge quantities of drugs of every kind. I swallowed them rapidly. She kept feeding me more saying, 'This will keep you stoned.'"

"This dream means far more than what it says from a literal standpoint," Vivian told them. "It is more lucid and logically ordered than most dreams, making it literal sounding, but always go beyond that for deeper meaning. The 'Far East' symbolizes wisdom. So it is a communication of wisdom from the realm of Spirit. Just as in our mundane world where often it is a crime to get caught possessing 'grass,' so, too, in the spiritual realm. The possession of 'grass' is a crime against Consciousness for Scripture tells us that 'grass' is fit for the oven to be burned."

"What is 'grass' in this sense?" a girl asked.

'Grass' is your <u>persona</u>," Vivian answered. "It is every attitude you have gathered from this life drama as to who you think you are in a literal sense. Your possession of it means 'death by hanging,' for it is a 'hang up' for Consciousness to be so attached to the personal sense of self as to forget Who and What It really is.

"In the dream this girl's physical 'father' stands for Conscious Causation. His statement, 'Eventually, everyone must die,' means that to claim your true identity you must 'die' to, or surrender, the personal sense of self. You must know that <u>you</u> are Consciousness. The girl's 'mother' stands for Mother nature, which, of course, can do nothing to rescue the personal sense. And the 'friend' stands for the literal mind, that which plies sleeping Consciousness with more and more hallucinations about Itself as something limited and finite, keeping it 'drugged,' or 'stoned,' for 'drugs' represent all the limited concepts Consciousness can identify with and be fixed in until It begins to awaken. To remain 'stoned' is to remain inert, to stay 'asleep,' instead of rousing Consciousness to Its true sense."

"Oh, wow!" I can see just where she is!" exclaimed the girl who had asked the question about "grass."

"Not where she is, but where Consciousness as her, is!" Vivian corrected. "Do you see what we're getting at here?"

Most of them gathered around her nodded readily, held in rapt attention by an account of a dream to which they could relate.

"I want you to understand one thing about dreams," Vivian went on. "Dreams, like myths and fairy tales, are blossoms on the same stem. They are cuttings from the same stalk. When I tell you to interpret your daily life as you do a dream, take everything within your compass as Consciousness displaying Its seven chief capacities in four modes of interpreting, and waking to Self-realization where It has been identified as the person you have called by your name.

"Dreams are characteristics of Consciousness made visible subjectively to each of us. But the same characteristics are also displayed in that which is objective to us, although there is nothing 'objective' to Consciousness. It's all subjective.

"I know that you're all familiar with *The Wizard of Oz*. M-G-M's version of L. Frank Baum's classic story, starring Judy Garland, is shown on television just about every year. I'd like you to remember what I see in it so you can look for that, too, the next time it is shown on TV."

By this time, those who had finished their coffee had taken their seats once more. Vivian waited until they were all reassembled before continuing. "The character, 'Dorothy,' played by Judy Garland," she said, "is the feminine of the masculine name, 'Theodore,' which means 'God's gift,' or grace of God. It is the personal sense of self that each of us has. It is our divine destiny to travel 'Over the Rainbow' to the true estate of the 'Emerald City.' 'Emerald,' being a shade of green, stands for the 'illumined mind.' The 'yellow brick road' is our line of life, our path through time in this physical world. We have with us on our journey several companions. The 'cowardly lion' symbolizes our fearful, physical instincts. The 'straw man' is the mind open only to literal thinking. The 'tin man' represents our lack of enlightened, positive emotion. Having no real Selfhood, we are empty, hollow, and tinny.

"The 'good witch' Dorothy encounters is our conscience, or intuitive faculty. The 'bad witch,' our paranoia, founded on the senses, that limits our identity to being a fragment that feels separate, and strives to gain power by exploiting what appears as 'others.' The 'poppy field' is the drugged sleep we have fallen into, in which all physical appearances entrance us into forgetfulness of being The Dreamer, and we believe ourselves to be 'one' among the

dreamt. 'Toto,' Dorothy's little dog, is the useful-
ness of personality, a faithful servant in this three-
dimensional world of ours when it is well-trained.
The 'Munchkins,' or dwarfs, are stunted develop-
ments. The 'ruby slippers' show that we are shod
for our journey and are protected by Love. The
'Wizard' is our Divine Self which has the power to
transform Itself into infinite definitions of Itself, and
to disengage from them at will."

With that she paused. Then after a few moments, "This is the typical format of all dreams.
When reduced to lesser levels of interpreting, based
on the personal sense of self, they lose their supreme
significance. Taken literally, that taking is what
Scripture refers to when it declares 'the letter killeth
the spirit.'"

Chapter 24

SEE YOUR DREAMS

FROM A HIGHER PERSPECTIVE

I noticed it was mostly women attending Vivian's dream classes and when I asked her about that she said, "Yes, I guess my groups contain only ten or twenty per cent men. The demands of their careers and making a living for their families is so absorbing that I don't see as many men here as I'd like. But when a man's dream world does begin to come alive, it often does so with great force--quite a shock--making him turn his attention away from externals and pay heed to what is happening inside himself."

"I had an experience like that," I offered.

"Good," she responded, "I'd like to hear about it."

"Well, I'll tell it to you. But first, I'd like to know if you can remember any outstanding dreams told to you recently by men?"

"Yes, I recall one that was told to me by a retired military man who came here one evening. He was a widower. In his dream he had moved into a small house after his wife died. He found himself in the foyer where there were several doors. One led to what he called his 'fishing room,' and another led

173

to the bedroom. He went through the fishing room and found himself in the kitchen. Then he found he couldn't get out of the kitchen. There was no way out of it. He wanted to go to his wife in the bedroom and he woke calling her name loudly, 'Bea! Bea!' he said. He repeated it, 'Bea! Bea! Bea!'"

Her recounting of it amused her. "Dreams love to use puns. I find them all the time," she chortled, "and it always casts characters in a scene that are appropriate to the dream theme. It is a subtle dream because the 'fishing room' represents the search for purpose. When Jesus said to his Disciples, 'I will make you "fishers of men"' it means more than going out and evangelizing the world. It doesn't mean to make proselytes for any ideology. It means one's 'disciples,' or one's trained disciplines, will 'fish out' meaning from all encounters in this life experience. You 'fish' for meaning in everything made manifest to you--every manifestation--that's what the 'men' in the 'fishers of men' mean."

"I follow you," I said.

"It's an instruction to you, the reader of the words in Scripture, to see experience from a higher perspective, as The Dreamer, not one of the dreamt," she emphasized. "After you've 'fished out' meaning from experience, what do you do with it? You transform it. So he went through his 'fishing room' to the kitchen, a room of transformation where raw materials are taken and refined through heat and cooking to turn them into more palatable substances. He could not get out of the place. He found himself sealed there, locked in. He wanted to join his wife who had greeted him and gone into another part of

174

the house. Finding himself locked away from her made him so frantic he woke up calling her name, 'Bea! Bea! Bea!'"

"That was a shock," I said.

"In more ways than one," she replied. "On the spiritual or divine level, it is expressive of the passion your Primal Self has for Its own reintegration and unification, to achieve or regain wholeness from Its fragmented state. A willful and joyful fragmentation, I might add, for as Blake said, 'Eternity is in love with the productions of Time.' It yearns to rouse us as Itself. God becomes Man that Man may become God. The way out of the locked room for the sleeper is just the way he came out of it crying, 'Be! Be! Be!' That's the second letter of the alphabet, and a small 'e,' his wife's name being a parody of that.

"Once you've gone through the 'fishing room' and have taken the meaning from manifestation, you're in the kitchen. Now you are to transform your impressions from literal to spiritual significance, interpreting from a new level of being. That crude, raw material must be refined and not be allowed to slip past you unattended all day long. Whatever you're confronted with all day in the life drama is not to be used to feed negative emotions. That isn't Christlike. You have to reconcile the world to your Self as it was said Jesus reconciled the world to himself. Of course, it's still going on and always has, because that's who you are. 'My Father and I are one,' he said. You and God are One. You just haven't come alive to it yet.

"As this man came out of the locked-in kitchen, he found himself saying, 'Be!' which signifies 'I am Being,' spelled with a capital 'B.' It's the only way out--when you transform meaning into Being."

"What did he think when you told him the dream's meaning?"

"He looked startled. His wife represents the Soul, and that is 'I Am,' and that is 'Be-ing.' He took in a breath and said, 'I never thought of it that way!' Such an impression bypasses literal minded-ness and registers with the spirit of That Which Is alive and present in all. It recognizes, when re-vealed, what It has always known, and that's what we feel so intently. We may not be able to formu-late it, but we feel it with intensity because divine Spirit Itself is roused in recognition when a dream is understood that way.

"The man reporting it to me took it literally, as the mass of humanity does. His wife portrays the Soul. And the only way you get out of the 'kitchen' is when you recognize your Soul is your Be-ing. That's the full transformation, but until that takes place you don't get out."

I was going to say something at this point but she didn't want me to speak just yet.

"His dream is one of the best in my collection. It is a small classic. And it calls to mind another equally classic dream, making almost the identical statement, that a woman reported to me some years ago. But what a difference in the outcome between the two!

"I call her dream 'The Cheaters' because it re-minds me of a story by that name on television. It was a story about a pair of spectacles, or 'cheaters,' that gave to all who put them on the power to discern the truth in all those around them, often with devastating effects. They got passed from one person to another until they finally came to a man who wasn't ready for them. His Soul asked him if he dared put them on. He said, 'Yes,' and when he did, he screamed in agony at what they showed him about himself. Our dreams often protect us, too, in shielding us from knowledge about ourselves that we aren't strong enough to bear--as I can show you--but I don't want to wander off, so back to the dream I call 'The Cheaters.'

"A woman said that in her dream she found herself in a closed room in a house and yet not of the house, but in a sealed room apart from the rest of it. There was a chest of drawers in this room, and above it, in a square frame, hung a mirror. There was a door on the right side of the room, sealed, too. On top of the chest were many pairs of sunglasses, of various colors. Someone spoke to her but she didn't see anyone. The voice said, 'Choose, for your release from this room depends upon how you choose.' Do you see the similarity here to the other dream? The closed room from which the single occupant could not escape?"

I nodded that I did. "How did she choose?"

"She told me she sorted through the pile of sunglasses and said, 'I can't choose any.' With that, presto! She awoke startled."

"What did you tell her?"

"I told her that the closed room is the mind of The Dreamer in the house of Consciousness. It's an

177

isolated room connected to the main structure, and the occupant is sealed in it. This means that Consciousness, The Dreamer, is focused in the realm of mental concepts, the 'chest of drawers' being the storage place of memories, opinions, judgments, and so forth, made from sensory data. Above the chest is a reflecting device, a mirror, showing The Dreamer current convictions of Self.

"She realizes her situation of being imprisoned in this isolated room. The voice of someone unseen is the Voice of Conscience and it commands her to act. The correct action through a careful discrimination will release her from the room. So she looks over the collection of pairs of glasses with their various colored lenses. 'Pairs' denote opposites and the profusion of many colors depicts multiplicity. When donned they obstruct the sun. This means 'hide, distort, veil, shade, and color' the sun. One pair or another, they are all alike in their altering the white light of Spirit.

"Her decision to choose among them for a pair of any sort would still be a blind. Conscience did not say, 'Choose a pair of glasses.' 'How you choose,' she was told, is what is important. Not to select any of the pairs of glasses, representing pairs of concepts made up of opposites, is the putting away of all that is seen and heard in the temporal sense-world. 'Coloring' is 'conditioning' Consciousness. This does not imply to suppress the body, mind, or feelings, but to take an unobstructed viewpoint.

"With that she woke immediately to find herself released from the room. Of course. That is the way to come out of your confinement to the mental, conceptual world. The doors open. Her Spiritual Identity has shown her how to be extracted from the unregenerate, colored states of mind.

"What both these dreams are requiring of us all is that we come out from appearances, of which we think we are but one among many, and see ourselves as The One Who Is Appearing, in numberless Self-definitions. In the man's case, he has this yet to do, while the woman has caught the spirit of it and is free now to grow consciously in her new Identity."

Chapter 25

YOUR DAILY DREAM

IS FOOD FOR GROWTH

I brought up a question about the man who woke from his dream calling, "Bea! Bea! Bea!" and Vivian's claim that it was a pun on the verb, 'to be,' and a cry of the dormant Self for Soul recognition.

"This kind of dream, it seems to me," I said, "would be difficult to get anyone to appreciate or understand other than on the literal level because, they'd probably think, 'The dream interpreter is merely extrapolating that for her own purpose.'"

"Oh, how many times have I heard someone say about my interpretation, 'That's your opinion.' Well, may I say, what other opinion can I have but mine?"

We both laughed.

"It would certainly be aped or copied, if I had any other, wouldn't it?" she asserted. "That always amuses me, because I could retort, 'It's your opinion that it's my opinion.' But, of course, that wouldn't get anywhere. We don't like to be disturbed. We don't like shocks. But I can't help it. It is not my 'person' that is doing it. And speaking of shocks, I believe you were about to tell me a dream of yours that woke you with a shock when we started this discussion about dreams that men have told me."

"Yes," I said, "it was short, but it really roused me because it was so real and what that reality meant. It woke me up with a shock, all right. It happened one night in spring after I'd been out helping take the County census. I would drive my car to my work area, park it in a shady place because the weather was hot, then take my clip board and work all around the block ringing doorbells and writing down answers to the census questions. I would then drive to the next block and repeat the whole process.

"That's what I was doing in my dream that night. It seemed as if I was right out there where I'd been working all day. I remember I came back to my car, got in and drove to the next area. It was hot weather. I was perspiring from walking. In this dream I was wearing my best suit of clothes, the only good suit I have. My car has leather seats and if I sit in it a long time when I'm hot and sweaty, my clothes stick to it. I didn't have my suit coat on in the dream as I had taken it off. But when I parked the car again and went to get out, I felt something rip. I put my hand under me and I could feel my bare skin. My trousers had stuck to the leather cushion and the seat had ripped out. I mean it was in shreds. And the shock of thinking I'd have to go on working the rest of the day with the seat of my pants gone, woke me up. They were my best trousers and I had no others to put on."

What I told her sent Vivian into gales of laughter. "I can't help it," she said after regaining her composure.

"It was so real," I said.

"I don't doubt it," she responded, "your inner Being was trying to tell you that all the convictions in which you have been 'seated' are worn out!"

"I see what you mean about puns."

"Oh, I think that's terrific," she said. "It tells me that the Being that you are has begun to stir from the long identification that it has made as your 'person.' I call it another example of an initiatory dream, and an excellent one. I'm glad you told it to me."

"I can tell you another that is even more of a shocker."

"Please do," she said with enthusiasm.

"Well, this dream happened not long after that. Maybe a couple weeks. In my dream I was indoors counting $58. worth of Fourth-of-July fireworks. They were in a large shipping box. Other people were in the house with me. The packing sheet listed skyrockets, pinwheels, and Roman candles amounting to $24. Those were the big items. I told the others present, 'Let's count all the little pieces first and the big stuff last.' When we got down to what was left, all I could find was four, red-white-and-blue-striped pieces with a fuse connecting them from top to bottom. There was a mistake, I thought. 'This can't be $24. worth,' I said, 'and it doesn't look like any skyrockets, pinwheels, or Roman candles I ever saw.' Then someone shouted at me, 'Look out! the fuse is lit!' 'Yes, don't let it go off in here!' the others cried. I wasn't alarmed. It was lit all right, sizzling and burning. 'I'll just pinch it out,' I said, and tried to do so, but the hot hissing fuse burned right under the pressure of my thumb--and the pain was excruciating! Seeing I wasn't able to pinch it out, I hurried to open the door. I did so and tossed the burning crackers into the air just in time. They went off with the most beautiful display of skyrockets, pinwheels, and Roman candles I ever saw!"

This got Vivian to laughing again.

"What's so funny? I can still feel the pain of that thing even now!"

"Oh, I know!" she said. "It's the way you describe it. I get the picture perfectly. Pardon me for laughing, but it shows what I know so well. When Consciousness decides to erupt from sleep, it really erupts! I'm going to add that to my collection. If I ever start a dream column, I'd like to use that one in it. May I?"

"Surely," I granted. Then she told me what it meant to her.

"The significance of both color and numbers is combined here. The dollar figure $58. stands for the total activity of Consciousness. Add the 'five' and the 'eight' and get 13. Then add the 'one' and the 'three,' reducing it to the number 'four.' 'Four' stands for the four functions of Consciousness. In the *Bible* it is the Four Rivers running out of Eden. Four-hundred years between the Old and the New Testaments. The Four Gospels. And numerous other indicators of the same.

"The large pieces in the box total $24. Add those two numbers and get 'six,' the sixth day of Creation, the day of Truth. The 'small stuff' has a value of $34. Those numbers add to 'seven' for the completion symbol, the seventh day of Creation. What July Fourth stands for is Independence Day! 'July' is the seventh month and the 'Fourth' is a national holiday, which to me means 'whole-"I"-day,' if you see the play on words here. It tells me it is a total emancipation from this dream we call life.

"You said the large pieces were strung together by a 'fuse.' To be 'fused' means to be connected, united in Consciousness. The 'four fire-crackers' in 'three colors' mean the completion of anything physical, or literal. "Red,' as you know, is Love. 'White' is Spirit. And 'Blue' is Truth. 'Red' and 'Blue' make 'Purple,' the kingly color of the Soul.

"The fuse is lit, meaning the activity of Consciousness is now alive and aware of Its own complete nature. You, as the Conscious Self in Its identification as your 'person,' not wishing to be destroyed, and desiring to be in control, try to snuff out the fuse, 'under the thumb.' But to be under the thumb of personality would be to be controlled by something inferior. The fuse burns through this obstruction.

"The live power of your inner Being erupts in a brilliant display of Its own elements for you. The Dreamer, as you, is released from all Its former Self-limited concepts. Your spiritual awakening is on. From now on your daily dream is food for the growth of Consciousness, so pay attention to what confronts you!"

Chapter 26

YOUR DAILY DREAM

IS FOOD FOR GROWTH

There is a responsive core deep in our emotions that comes vibrantly alive at times when important communication is transmitted to us. It makes your skin tingle like a sharp charge of electricity running through you. You can feel your hair rise along your scalp. I get that way listening to the crackling dialogue of a Rod Serling television drama because he had the rare gift of being attuned to inner wisdom. Truth from such a source is well recognized and responded to by the Truth within ourselves in rare moments of ultra-high-frequency communication.

That is what Vivian's interpretation of my dreams do for me. Admittedly for others, too, I have heard them say. And it was never experienced more intensely than when she gave me her insight into my Independence Day dream.

Having a dream like that and hearing it interpreted in the way I did made me feel lit up for days. "The memory of that dream," I said to her, "is as vivid now as those of any Fourth-of-July fireworks celebrations I witnessed along the river banks of my youth. Anytime at all, I can bring back that dream memory to the very last sparkler, no less than the memory recall of ice cream, lemonade, cannon crackers, bunting-decked platforms for Fourth-of-July speeches, and patriotic parades that ever took place in my waking world. I can still feel that burning fuse under my thumb!" I shook it at her and treated her to a look of pain.

"So where does fantasy end and reality begin?" she said laughing. "Truly, the real world is that of the imagination in comparison to which this world is but fleeting forms and passing shadows."

"I am reminded of something James Michener said," I replied. 'We are like stones thrown into water, wet on the surface, but not a part of the water.' Having a dream like my Fourth-of-July dream is like having a hard casing break loose all around you. You find yourself absorbed into something bigger than you can remember you were before, It flowing into you, you flowing into It. The effect on me of what you said was electric."

"That is because it did not come from my 'person,'" she said. "An unfertilized egg will be an unfertilized egg forever, but once fertilized, a chick begins to grow. To me, a dream such as the one you've just told me, is evidence of that fertilization. Something can now grow within you that was not able to before that moment. Now it's a matter of your nurturing it and feeding it properly."

"Will my ability to understand my dreams grow, too?"

"It should. I find it happening among several I know who have attended my groups. I am thinking in particular of a woman who came from England. She had once met Gurdjieff at his chateau on the outskirts of Paris. She was a young girl at the time but she remembers meeting him. In the spring of 1974, some fifty years later, she had this dream:

"'I went to a meeting of Gurdjieff's students,' she told me. 'I was wearing pink slippers. We all sat down to a meal that consisted of a buttered bread-roll, each. I told them I had been sent by Gurdjieff to see how they were getting on. But they paid no attention to me and went on talking among themselves. I said no more and left, thinking there was no love in this group.'

"When I asked her what she had gotten from her dream, she replied, 'Love resides in the higher center, the true "I." Only God can know God. The pink slippers represent the combining of Love and Spirit that clothe the understanding. The meal is a eucharistic one, a feast of love, but the multitude of "I's" in us do not know this. "They have made my house a den of thieves," Scripture says. True "I" has given Its substance to feed the many "I's," then It separates Itself.'

"I get more from her dream than what she gave me at that moment, but that is excellent. You should be able to do as well as that, too, given time for the faculty to mature."

"I call it simply, 'insight.' It shows forth in that woman's dream as well as in her handling of it. The faculty of 'insight' being an indicator of 'awakened Man,' the figure of Gurdjieff in her dream represents in the psyche of Man, that which is instructive in spiritual awakening, this being the life role he played at Fontainbleu as the head of The Institute for the Harmonious Development of Man which he founded in the early part of the twentieth century.

"This world of ours is like a squirming larvae bed. True humanity grows out of it, not into it. Spiritual Identity when lost in Its identifications cannot know Itself as Itself. It takes the Self to awaken the Self. In this woman's dream she is 'The Word' that is sent by The Sender. She plays the role of the Soul aspect of Consciousness--that which evaluates--for this is what she does all through the dream. Her understanding is one of inner light for what she wears on her feet are slippers, not a heavy footing for literal trodding like shoes. As she says, they signify that in her understanding she is supported by Love. 'Bread' is literal food. To eat of it, spiritually, is to discern what it contains, to extract meaning from life's manifestations. A 'buttered bread roll' implies a richness of this substance, and, indeed, the life activity going on around us every day is filled with richness, if we can 'break' such 'bread' and extract its inner meaning. Those who eat of it in her dream do not respond to her statement about her being sent to see how they are getting on. The 'multitude' is unaware of, and not conversant with, unity. Consequently, the Soul--The Dreamer--withdraws, knowing there is no way of establishing rapport with them. She is the fullness of Love. They are only illustrations of Love's activity."

I was impressed. "That's pretty heavy stuff," I said.

"It's the essence of what our dreams are saying when taken on the highest level of meaning, but it depends on an inner faculty enlivened enough to see it."

"If you were to epitomize the subject of dreams in a sentence or two, what would you say?" I asked.

"You can pose some tough ones," she rejoined. "Dreams show me either the extremity of Self-forgetfulness, or varying stages of recovery from that forgetfulness. That's it in a nutshell. Or rather, an eggshell, this world being a spiritual incubator for the growth of Consciousness. A chick grows from the yolk of an egg. The white of the egg serves as its food while it is maturing enough to break out of the shell. That dream of yours of your trousers being in shreds is what I call an initiatory dream. It means that Consciousness is stirring from Its long sleep where It has been identified as the one you have been calling by your name."

"It came on me without any warning," I said.

"It invariably does!" she cried. "Scripture tells us that it comes like a 'thief in the night.' While we are on the bed in our dreams, the old sense of self is snatched away. As the Book of Job says, "in slumberings upon the bed the ears of men are opened and their instruction sealed." Consciousness does what man cannot do. Your job is to identify as That. Begin practicing living as That. To do so, you need a special kind of food."

"Food?"

"Yes, food. Oh, not the store kind. Or what you raise in a garden. It is what you've been feeding on all your entire life but little of it has gone to feed and nourish Conscious Awareness. It has been nourishing your life as <u>persona</u>, Consciousness shut down in sleep."

"In my groups I make use of the *Psychological Commentaries on the Teachings of Gurdjieff and Ouspensky*, by the late Maurice Nicoll, a doctor-pioneer in psychological medicine during World War I. He studied with Gurdjieff at Fontainbleu, France, after the war, and gave up a lucrative practice in London's Harley Street to write those *Commentaries*. Times almost without number he writes about what he calls the 'food of impressions,' meaning all that we take in all day long in the way of ideas. Sleeping humanity is only about half-conscious of what it takes in, and most of all that goes to feed our negative emotions. Negative emotions kill conscious growth. That is why such things as 'repentance' and 'forgiveness' are so important, except that there is more meaning in those words and what they imply for us than simply feeling sorry for our conduct, or excusing others for theirs. Unless we really change, inwardly, and radically so, feeling badly about our shortcomings isn't of much use."

Chapter 27

YOUR DAILY DREAM

IS FOOD FOR GROWTH

"When it comes to how we are feeding ourselves, spiritually," Vivian said, "I am reminded of a dream by a man in his forties. In it he saw several loaves of bread and all of his elder brother's writings were printed on the bread wrappers. But he ignored them as food. Instead, he took a *National Geographic* magazine, placed it in a frying pan over a fire and began to saute it.

"His elder brother is a writer, but in this dream his brother's writings are a symbolic reference to the words of Christ, meaning our Gospels, for 'Jesus Christ' is everyman's elder brother. It is the sayings of Christ passed down to us that provide food for soul growth. 'Bread' represents nourishment from Heaven, the illumination of Consciousness, and provides sustenance for one who is hungry. But the subject doesn't see that as value. He is looking for something else to feed on and decides to cook the *National Geographic* magazine, which stands for everything in the literal, physical, sense-based, factual world. And without meaning any detraction to this excellent magazine, it is just pulp, in the spiritual sense. The magazine's yellow cover is clue here to that fifth aspect of Consciousness, Life, whose color and symbol is a golden-yellow cross. If we don't feed on the 'bread' of Heaven, we feed on 'pulp,' which doesn't feed the soul.

"Read the first four verses of the sixth chapter of the Book of Acts, but take what you read off the literal level. It sounds like a discussion of the division of labor. Who is going to minister unto the widows of the Greeks? And who is going to conduct God's work, the prayer ministry? The decision is made in the third verse where it says, 'Wherefore, brethren, look ye out among you seven men of honest report whom we may appoint over this business.'

"The business referred to is that of handling life impressions with which you deal every day. You need men-servants of honest report, mental department heads, who can be relied on to sort and classify all incoming impressions, ordering them properly-- judging 'righteous judgment' the Scriptures say--that you may grow consciously through this practice, instead of following the reactive, self-serving, wishy-washy entity called persona which is so unstable as to scarcely merit being called an entity. It is a complex of sense-based convictions you've built up as your identity. To serve True Identity, you call on the seven aspects of Consciousness.

"The woman who knew Gurdjieff had another short dream that applies here. In it, someone had stolen a washing machine from her apartment. She complained to the manager who brought the police. While they were looking around the apartment, the thieves returned, and the police captured them and took them away. To me, the 'washing machine' symbolizes purification equipment. The negative emotions steal it every chance they get. They have access to our incoming impressions and take what is valuable, our energy, our force. But in this subject's case they are held, and revealed, by the disciplinary functioning of the Self, the 'police.' It is a good dream report and the kind I'm glad to hear. The culprits are caught. They are disclosed. They are made known, and they are held. She knows Who she is, and how to function. This dream verifies it!

"The 'seven men of honest report' cited in Acts are referred to as the 'seven churches' in Revelation. In the 12th chapter of 1st Corinthians, verse 28, Paul designates them 'diversities of tongues,' but lists them in reverse order to the way they are stated in Genesis. Named last is the 'diversities of tongues' and the ability to interpret them. This signifies Mind with all its amazing constructions. Next is 'helps' and 'governments,' the governor being Principle, leading to mastery. Again, following this reverse order, 'healings' are mentioned. What heals you is recognizing your source, your essential Self as Spirit. After that comes the 'miracles.' You're the 'miracle worker' when you have learned to translate the mundane into the sacred for the word, 'religion,' means to relate to Cause. Yoga means yoke to Cause, the activity of the Soul. Paul then names 'teachers' and your 'teacher' is Life. Everything that Consciousness is contemplating is dramatized and personified. When you can see that, you make Life your teacher. Proceeding upward once more, we find what Paul calls 'prophets.' A 'prophet' is that function of Consciousness which reveals Truth at whatever density or intensity level Consciousness is focused on. Lastly, but named first, are 'apostles.' An 'apostle' is one who recognizes his divinity through direct experience. That is the aspect of Love, the completed state of Self-discovery where one knows his essential Self to be God. The only difference is one of degree.

"One day," she continued, "a good student of mine, a young black woman who had been in class, called me on the telephone. 'I had a good "Three-D" experience,' she said--which is the way we talk about the events in our daily waking dream--'but I don't get it. I went along with my father to a magic store in San Francisco, a voodoo shop, where they sell amulets. He thought if he had them he could re-member something he'd forgotten that was impor-tant to him. But when he got home he didn't know how to line them up and make them work.'

"I said to her, 'Isn't that delightful! The seven days of Creation, the capacities of Consciousness, are each one's amulets. Remember my vision of the Tree, the Pyramid, the Diamond, and so forth? We all have them but don't know how to line them up. We are trying to make contact not with something outside ourselves but qualities of our own nature that are always with us. Asleep, we go searching for them but they are right with us all the time and we don't know their function. They are like fulcrums, points of balance between opposites. When some-thing is presented to us by the actions and interac-tions of the characters in our daily dramas, we should stand on these fulcrums so that we are not caught by either of a pair of opposites. To remain consciously 'awake' all day and not fall in the mire of negative emotions, you must bring up something between you and every incoming impression right at that instant and reconcile it under Mind, Principle, Spirit, Soul, Life, Truth, and Love.'

"Every dramatic presentation has a theme-- maybe several--arising from the behavior of those who interact with us, by what they say and show to us. When we have identified that theme we have to call up its opposite, or its complement, within ourselves and find the appropriate aspect of Consciousness on which to stand, like a fulcrum, so that we are not caught emotionally in either extreme of it.

"'Everyone of us has his amulets right with him,'" I told her, 'and their purpose is to help us remember our Godhood. But just like your father, we don't know how to use them for recollection!'"

"That's a good one," I said, "isn't it?"

"It was for me," she returned. "Marvelous. They are with us always but we forget what they represent."

"Why would a man go to a magic store," I said, to get some amulets and then after getting them not know what to do with them? What was he trying to do?"

She broke me up replying, "If he had known that, we wouldn't have the story, would we?" and her burst of laughter overshadowed mine.

"It sounds like a little kid," I chuckled.

"It is a little kid. She said to me in class, 'My parents seem like children to me.'"

In discussing it further, Vivian said, "The idea that comes out in fairy tales about an amulet, or talisman--something you tie on a string or chain and wear on your person--is a good one because all of us are looking for something we can clutch and cling to in times of stress. Whether it is something physical to place in the pocket, or something to remember, we'd like to have an amulet that is foolproof in its working power.

"When an impression comes from that which we call external--another person, or from an environmental situation--if you find yourself flooded with feelings of irritation, annoyance, objection, and resentment over this particular thing, practice asking yourself whether it is directed, personally, at you. Do this for the sake of discernment, of classifying it, 'yes' or 'no.' If it's 'no' and you still find feelings of resentment arising, then you must recognize there is something in you that you haven't gotten at. When directed at you, personally, and you rise in opposition, this is a natural defense reaction. Our persona always defends itself against all onslaughts, even though in the deeper recesses the accusation may be correct. But when it's not levelled at you, when it's not personal, and you see irritation and objection coming up, then you have to say, 'Behind this is really something I have to look for in myself.'"

Chapter 28

YOUR DAILY DRAMA

IS FOOD FOR GROWTH

"To feed yourself Conscious food," Vivian went on, "you identify each impression as the function of one or more of your seven aspects, or capacities, performing properly or awake, or improperly asleep, as the case may be. You don't allow yourself to get worked up over that which you, The Observer, see functioning. If you do, you lose force and waste energy. You can't grow that way. You come out of the life 'dream' and the same kind of behavior performed by those in it by positioning yourself as The Dreamer, no longer just one of the dreamt. You see every last manifestation as the activity of all seven of your aspects, some more prominently displayed and at work than others in the various incidents of daily life, but all of them bound in dynamic relationship to each other.

"In Gurdjieffian parlance this is called 'remembering yourself.' Dr. Maurice Nicoll calls it 'The Work.' Its what you do morning, noon, and night from now on. You put your seven men of honest report, your seven aspects, right between the incoming impression and the ordinary reaction that would usually take place, behaving as one of the characters in your dream. The watchword is constant vigilance. You have to be prepared for anything, anytime. Try not to be taken unaware."

"How do you keep your guard up all the time?"

"That's the challenge. It's easy to slip into the same old well-worn role, the habit of letting everything hit you as one among many who has to defend himself against them all."

"How do you do that all day long?"

"By turning it into habit. Like all habits, old ones are hard to get rid of. I try to remind myself, 'Where irritation begins, Consciousness ends.' And another one, 'Where no offense is taken, none can be given.' Think about that. And impress yourself with it. There's a darn good amulet for you, if that's what you're looking for. Mentally carve it on a piece of jade, hang it around your neck and see yourself reading it back to yourself many times a day. Eventually, it will be on the surface of your awareness at all times. It will be there when you need it. I'm not in favor of handing out crutches. I've heard it said, we inherited crutches and then lost faith in our legs. All of us have to find our own private way of insulating ourselves against everything that would take our force from us, stunting the growth of the precious, small thing in ourselves that is seen so often as the 'babe' or the 'child' in our dreams. Each of us has to do his own maturing. No one can do it for us. But we can tell others what it is that we find works for us, and let them judge for themselves.

"When you become so in love with your innate Spiritual Identity--the Christ Child in the manger born--that absolutely nothing else can rise that high and supplant it in your affection, then, indeed, can no offense be taken, or given--" she paused to touch my arm, "--the 'manger' being just this animal form you find yourself wearing. You experience the birth of that Child while you are inhabiting this fleshly form. That, to me, is the real meaning of the Christmas Story, for I've experienced it. God, being no respecter of persons, there is no reason why you won't experience it, as you will--as all will--for that is destiny. 'My word shall not return unto me void,' our Scriptures say.

"This 'new birth' is but the beginning. We have to strengthen that Child, mature it. We must enter into a long schooling in which no one is the task master but ourselves. Everything that would ordinarily seize us and eat our force has to be mastered. What are these things? We have to identify them for ourselves, using our seven good men to neutralize them and release them. Making the day pass this way is the way to becoming unbound and free."

"It's not something that sounds easy."

"No. And the gymnasium gets tougher as you move through it. Take what the day delivers to you, no more and no less than that. This is called living 'in the moment,' not 'for the moment.' The purpose is to expand Consciousness through this reconciling involvement with your 'waking dream.' Your work is in this daily drama, not heading for a cave, or the Himalayas, as an escape. You have to overcome every handicap along the course, determining with all your resolve to do it, weak as you are. By adding to your Self-knowledge you build that 'New Jerusalem.'

Nothing can take your understanding from you. In our old, sense-based way of thinking from our customary mental and emotional sets, we judged from appearances, from effects made manifest, by that shape, by that form. Seeing newly, we judge what the shape, the effect, is conveying in terms of the aspects of Consciousness."

"If we're reacting we can't do it?"

"No, and if you are truly reconciling, you won't be reacting since our pin-point minds can only focus on one thing at a time. If you focus on being Consciousness, then you are that. It saves you from going down 'into the pit.' By remembering yourself as Consciousness, right at the point of incoming impressions, you erect an impregnable wall. You become immunized from everything in life that would consume your force. You conserve it by directing it inward to the very core of your being, to Cause, not wasting it out there on the periphery where Cause is only seen as effect. If you react, you lose force. If you remain neutral, you conserve force. If you reconcile, you increase force. That's the work you do all along the road to 'awakening,' and the food for that work is everything transpiring in your daily 'dream.'"

"You say you have to focus on being Consciousness?"

"Yes. Everything that appears is a definition Consciousness makes of Itself. Think of what the Orientalist says, 'The wrong man with the right tools will create a wrong result.' So you think you are going to <u>be</u> Buddha? You are the wrong man for you can't <u>become</u> Buddha. You have to start <u>from</u>

Buddha, <u>from</u> Christ, <u>from</u> Krishna, or whatever. Then you're the 'right' man. We must start from the epitome. We must remember that Consciousness has two poles, in our western world Adam and Christos. The 'fall' and the 'redemption.' But It is the Selfsame One dramatized in these two viewpoints. Unless I identify as the total of It, how can I reach It? That's Scriptural for it says, 'The Jews took up stones to stone him,' for he, being a man, declared himself to be God, and such a declaration was considered blasphemy. But it's really the other way around for it's blasphemy to declare your 'person' to have reality independent from its source. So unless you believe, 'I am He,' you die in your sins for unless that can be acknowledged, the door is shut."

"You die in your thought?"

"You are 'dead' already because you have missed the mark. To 'miss the mark' being the translation of the Greek word, to 'sin,' and to sin in the ultimate is never to find out who you are. There is no separation between you and the world but it's hard to be convinced of the truth of that without what is called a mystical experience. So you have to take it on trust, first as an intellectual proposition. Make that assumption, 'I am He,' and abide in it continually. Tell yourself that subject-and-object thinking is always the occupation of being one among the dreamt. That isolates you. That keeps you insecure. Consequently, that keeps you defensively reactive. The Dreamer is not caught in this dichotomy when He knows He's dreaming. Everything to The Dreamer is subjective because He is all. So position yourself as That in your movement about

203

the daily 'dream.' Find ways not to lose that position by telling yourself, 'What I am beholding is Consciousness beholding Itself in the imagery by which It understands Itself.' Got it?"

"Got it," I responded, hoping and feeling that I truly had.

Chapter 29

YOUR "PERSON"

IS NOT THE DREAMER

"Much as I try to do as you say and focus on being Consciousness," I told Vivian, "I don't like the idea of being wiped out as a person."

"You can't lose anything by losing what you aren't."

"No? I remember a saying, 'He who stands for nothing will fall for everything.'"

"That's true, but you don't become 'nothing' by giving up your personal sense as your identity. What you do is take your stand as unconditioned Consciousness. When you do that, when you stand as 'no thing' you will not fall into anything. What you see in the world may not be your responsibility, but how you treat it in you, is. Nicoll, in his *Commentaries*, says that 'unless the grip of personality is weakened, no psychological transformation is at all possible.'[7] That's how you weaken it--through <u>metanoia</u>--that radical turnaround the Scriptures tell us to make. Take up a new position. Identify as Consciousness. The mechanical effects you now see around you every day are the expression of your

---

[7] Nicoll, Vol. III, p. 1051.

seven aspects. 'Awake,' as Consciousness, you won't be inclined to behave as one of the dreamt. If you don't fall into states by tripping over the same old re-embodied portrayals every time they come a-round, you've expanded Consciousness. You're at a different level of being than before. Remember the dream of the man who woke calling, 'Be! Be! Be!'"

"He said he was calling his wife, Bea."

"That's from the personal sense view. Your 'person' isn't The Dreamer. During physical sleep, Consciousness is no longer focused on the sense-based world. The bed, and even the body resting on it, is wiped out, Consciousness having withdrawn from one level to another, the core of Itself, which in Scripture is called Heaven. Then occurs what is called a dream. The dream may make some refer-ence to what you know as your daily world, but it has no relevance to it for your 'person' isn't in it. It lies immobilized on the bed. In the dream, Con-sciousness brings together actors to play out themes of Its own choosing without regard as to what you, as 'person,' might like or not like. Persona has nothing to say about it. An elderly woman told me a dream in which she found herself in her attic, looking over all the things she had collected during her life. Box after box was filled with these effects and she was going through all of them. But she couldn't bring herself to part with any of them because it was all so precious to her.

"At that moment, the Salvation Army in full force came marching in. They picked up everything and moved toward the door. She stopped them saying, 'That's mine!' They did, putting down the boxes and departing. She was left clinging to her sentimentality.

"I'll give you another dream illustrating this," she went on. "It came from a technical editor in the aerospace industry. It was morning. He stepped out onto his porch and climbed a double flight of stairs to get his mail. He found a package stamped 'Fourth Class,' labeled 'Occupant.' The address was correct, however, so he took it down into the house. He opened it. Inside were two books with covers of a rich velour fabric. One was blue, the other, red, stamped in Roman numerals, 'VI,' and 'VII.' He noticed they were the collected works of Plato and he stroked their soft covers with his hands.

"What this dream shows me is an ascension to a high level of communication, signified by the mail box at the top of the stairs. The 'Fourth Class' package illustrates balance in the fourfold modes of Self-interpreting. 'Books' symbolize knowledge and volumes 'six' and 'seven' show works of wisdom and power. 'Blue,' number six, is wisdom. The other, 'red,' number seven, is power. In ancient times a philosopher was a lover of wisdom, personified in this dream as 'Plato.' The 'hands' contacting the books shows the power to grasp these high ideals. The subject noted the package was not addressed to him, showing that the works of Truth and Love do not belong to his <u>persona</u>. No acknowledgement is made of 'persons' for Consciousness can only give recognition to Itself. And that is Scriptural, 'For there is no respect of persons with God.' Does this help to convince you Who You Are?"

"I don't deny that it does. But it's such an audacious claim."

"The veil of physicality hides Consciousness. The Whole phenomenal universe is the veil and we sleep as 'Adam' beneath it, having abandoned the primal sense of Self. We are so small in our sense of ourselves as 'persons' that we try to enlarge this sense of attachment--as shown by the elderly woman's 'attic' dream. To recover your divinity, you must first discover it. To discover it, assume it. Begin with the assumption and it will end with the realization. God assumes Man and Man must resume God, for that is what He is at the opposite end of His conception of Self. Life is a mirror and an echo chamber. What you haven't yet accepted in yourself, as well as what you have confirmed in your conviction of yourself, is constantly being made visible and audible to you, Consciousness, and that is all that is going on. Begin to see One-Self in all things, and all things in One's Self, instead of 'me' and 'it.'"

"Our daylight experience is just as much a dream as our nighttime experience then, isn't it?" I queried.

"Yes, in that like a night dream it has no permanence. When we are in what we call our everyday waking state we know that dream states exist because we have the memory of them. But when we are dreaming, we do not know that this 'waking' world exists. Each state has its own reality while Consciousness is focused in it, forgetful of the other. And because most of us have had no experience of that state called 'Cosmic Consciousness,' we can't appreciate that our present daily world is like a night dream seen from a higher intensity.

"In the twentieth verse of the 73rd Psalm we read, 'As a dream when one awaketh; so, O Lord, when thou awakest.' To me, the difference between this waking, three-dimensional dream we share together, and the dream of the night, is that when you wake from the latter you sometimes recall you were dreaming, with varying degrees of vagueness or sharpness. But in the night dream you never recall the three-dimensional state with any memory, vague or sharp. Therefore, you believe the night dream to be unreal when you recall it. But while having the night dream the question doesn't arise. It is your reality for you while you are in it. And like in your night dream, while you are awake in the world you cannot conceive of another reality that would make this one fade as your night dream does when you awake from it. Sometimes in bed, you have the experience of knowing that you are dreaming--the so-called 'lucid' dream--and you rise recalling it all. To wake out of this three-dimensional world would be just like that. It is something we are all destined to do, I am certain. Dreaming is, therefore, a foreshadowing of this.

"Dreams are the language of one's essential being in the discovery of Itself. Dream images are seemingly related to your external world because these images are often of familiar people, places and things of which you are aware. But a dream, to me, is an impartial statement of The Dreamer's Self-knowledge. I don't say a 'person's self-knowledge because 'persons' are definitions of the invisible

Conscious Awareness of Being. This takes them off the level of most psychologists and their premise that there are separate and multiple dreamers. It seems so. But then it has been said, 'That which seems to be, is, to those to whom it seems to be.' Or, to put it another way, "If you don't understand, things are just as they are. If you do understand, things are just, as they are."

"The One Dreamer can be called God, Brahman, Allah, Christ, Buddha, The Tao, or any term signifying Infinity. This is the basis of all genuine religion: wherever Consciousness is claiming identity as 'I,' is where the living reality of Infinity is declaring Its presence.

"You and Infinity are One. Dreams are an essential dynamic given to us to communicate that process and its stages to those who understand. Prayer and dreams are opposite poles of one communication. Prayer is the restricted pole of Selfhood trying to contact its source. Dreams are the source trying to make contact with the restricted Selfhood. The purpose of dreaming is to bring sleeping Man to a point of internal awareness.

"The Dreamer is The Revealer and The Dreamer is One. You can establish this to your satisfaction. When you awaken from a dream in the morning reflect on the question, 'Who was there in the dream?' You may have seen familiar faces--perhaps world-famous persons--but did any of them know they appeared in your dream? No. So how many had knowledge of the dream? Just one. That One is You, The Dreamer of it all. Is this too audacious for you to accept? If it is, you will never reach true dominion as long as you hold a lesser feeling."

"But all around me I see others, so I must be a 'part' and each of them must be a 'part.'"

"Yes, and that is what you see in the dream of the night, too. You see many others. All are parts being played. But there in Only One Player. When the dream is over they all disappear but The One who wakes to find He played them all. You were the only life that any of those dream figures had. Understanding what the night dream is saying--that you are The Dreamer--and interpreting the incidents of the active, daily, three-dimensional 'dream' from this new perspective should convince you that you are more than an infinitesimal speck of humanity among billions of others and set you on the course to freedom as the Self, revealing Itself to Itself unto Infinity."

Chapter 30

LIFE IS A DREAM

FROM WHICH ALL AWAKE

"There is more interest in dreams today than ever before," Vivian told me. "It is a part of the current quest for self-knowledge and the expansion of consciousness growing in intensity."

"Newspapers have picked up on it," I said, "magazine writers, too. Persons from many fields are turning out books on dreams but few of them touch the subject the way you do. Much of it is mishmash and a lot of it complex and confusing. How do you feel about that?"

"The letter killeth," she said. "Taking dreams literally is like taking parables literally. When a thing of spiritual value is reduced to the mundane, it loses its deeper intent. Anyone with a *Bible* background knows Jesus spoke to the multitude in parables--and still does--for that's what dreams are. But no one can see this for another. Each has to see it for himself, or miss it. You can't borrow understanding. You have to cultivate your own. Sincere scholars are trying to find greater meaning in dreams than academic research has yielded thus far. I wish them well. The *Talmud* says, 'A dream which is not understood is like a letter which is not opened.'

What I am trying to do is point in a direction that has scarcely been followed, the spiritual direction. It is a mystery to me why modern scholars with few exceptions are so reluctant to look in that direction. Wherever dreams are studied today, the Talmudic dictum is being overlooked. It certainly doesn't enter into the studies of sleep laboratories. Because of reduced brain wave activity during sleep, dreams are regarded as a form of low-grade thinking. That isn't very Talmudic.

"Then, of course, when any subject that researchers are probing reaches public attention the publishing industries are quick to exploit it for profit. So we have a lot of people who are sounding off on the subject without due regard to what effect they are having on the readers of newspapers, magazines, and books.

"To trust the dream interpretations of anyone, where such are levelled negatively by creating suspicion, envy, lust, animosity, and fear toward persons whose familiar images appear in dreams is foolish. The one who accepts such interpretations regresses rather than going forward to greater mental and emotional maturity. By harboring mistaken beliefs that are given to you in ignorance, you limit yourself, you bind yourself, you corrupt your attitudes toward others. Instead of becoming more stable, more loving, you lose psychological and spiritual ground. You deny yourself the opportunity for developing the soul, which is what dreams are meant to do.

"Dreams act in your best interest and the actions of people whom you know who show up in your dreams are meant to show you things about yourself that you should work on internally, and not react to, literally. Then you can profit, for dreams have benign intentions no matter how frightening. Don't surrender the sovereignty you have over your own mind and feelings by succumbing to negative opinions about others that anyone tries to make you accept. If you do, to the extent that you do, they own you like a hypnotist owns you, if you submit your will to his. False instruction will lead you to project a feeling of resentment and others will behave accordingly, if that is what you are convinced of in your heart. Don't be afraid of anything you dream. Therefore, don't shy away from dream recall no matter how repulsive to you the dream may have seemed. Our dreams are not given to us as a varnish, an agreeable reflective coating for our fictions about ourselves. Instead, they show us the unvarnished truth. The purpose of a dream is to wake us out of a psychological state, not to keep us in it. If you can find the import of your dream symbols beyond signifying relationships with other persons in your mundane affairs and bring them to conscious identification and acceptance, you will have set yourself on the road to inner freedom. If not, you remain in their thrall until you do. Dreams are heralds of states we are in or are passing through. So to understand your dreams is to know where you are in Spirit. Their relevance to our mundane affairs, while not impossible--as witness some of the great inventions and classic stories that have come from dreams, is so far beneath their genuine significance as to be hardly worth noting.

"A dream is something that enables you to put yourself in touch with yourself. Always break that last word in two. Capitalize the 's,' and you have it: your 'Self.' You never were apart from it. It only seemed so. I sometimes illustrate this for my classes by the use of an ordinary kitchen colander. With holes, you know?"

"Yes, I know."

"I hold it up in front of the light from a floor lamp and ask the students to look at the light pattern on the carpet formed by its passing through the colander holes. 'You never were anything but the light,' I tell them, 'even though you may identify as one of those tiny spots of light, affixed as you are to your human body.' It's a graphic way I've found of putting across the point that you could not have come into physical existence without Consciousness coming with you, surrendering Its primal abode to 'enter death's door,' as William Blake put it. To 'lose' Its life in order to take on yours."

"That seems to be another way of saying what we hear from the pulpits of Christian churches, that Jesus 'died' for all humanity."

"You're right. That's the deeper meaning of the saying that Christ died on the cross to save Man. The human body is the 'cross' on which Jesus 'dies,' or, as I say, to which Consciousness affixes Itself until the dream of life is over. When it is, you will be restored to your True Identity. In good time. You can delay it or accelerate it. But you can't prevent it, for 'you,' as person, aren't doing it.

"How do you delay it?"

"By not recognizing, or being indifferent to the unitary nature of being."

"And how do you accelerate it."

"By recognizing that your being and God's being are one and the same. There is no separation in Consciousness, only in physical formulation. Here, on this plane, we are now individualized in the flesh. Destiny is to become spiritually individualized when all the opposites of this world have been known."

"Meaning everyone of us?"

"Everyone. 'Not one shall be lost in all my holy mountain,' sayeth the Lord. And elsewhere in Christ's words, 'It is the Father's will which hath sent me, that all of which he hath given me I should lose nothing.' You wake from every dream state, including this 'dream' called Life. You do not know how many states you have embraced thus far. Nor do you suspect how many until the process of your spiritual awakening begins. The characters of Scripture are personifications of these states through which we pass. When we have passed through the last of these, which the *Bible* calls, 'the day of Jesus Christ,' our journey in this world is over and we are restored to the Divine perspective, which was 'before the world was.' In our present state, we have no life in ourselves. We are animated forms. We are individualized in the flesh. But destiny is to be individualized in Spirit, priests forever 'after the order of Melchizedek,' according to the Psalmist, 'Melchizedek' being the prototype of Christ. We are not yet 'whole,' but we shall be. To achieve wholeness, admit to the truth of what your dreams are saying at the deepest level, the symbolic level. This is often distasteful, it is painful, to discover you aren't the strong and courageous, the great and noble, sincere and beautiful entity you thought you were. Presently, you aren't an 'entity' at all. You are a bundle of conflicts, a collection of contradictions, a mass of small 'I's,' as the late Dr. Maurice Nicoll declared. You have no undiminishable, indissoluble, permanent 'I,' but that is the direction in which Your Inner Being is moving, and your dreams are Its report as to how far along the road to integration It presently is where It is identified as you."

"To dismiss dreams at other levels than this is to miss their import and remain psychologically unintegrated. Your rational mind may scoff at this and deny it, but scoffing and denial don't offset it. Until you can accept what your dreams are saying as the essential truth about you, right at this moment in the depths of Being, you are living in a dream world more impermanent than the one you enter at night."

"How do you say we should advance the integrative purpose and process of dreams?"

"By active participation. That participation begins with your admission that you have no 'inner' integrity. Oh, you may be one who pays his bills, who wouldn't cheat anybody. Well and good but it's more than that. When you can honestly admit to and accept those dream symbols that are saying, 'You have no inner integrity,' you are helping to clear the ground for its construction. The time to make this discovery about yourself is here, now, in this life. Have you heard the story about a man, who, curious about reincarnation had himself re-gressed through hypnotism and found that he was dead in another life? Well, he's dead in this life, too, until he is redeemed."

"Who are the redeemed?"

"The redeemed are those who have returned to the knowledge of their Divine Identity while in the flesh. Scripture defines only two states of being, the 'quick' and the 'dead.' The *Bible* does not say that God is a God of the dead but of the living. Which means that God is dead only if you are. Appearing as encapsulated in flesh, you think of your discrete-ness accordingly. But remember the lamplight shin-ing through the perforated colander. Essentially, you aren't one of those little spots of light. You are The Totality individualizing Itself. What you are claiming as your present, personal identity is a Self-imposed restriction."

Vivian told me, finally, of a small boy who re-turned home from Sunday School and said to his fa-ther, "If God loved us so much, why didn't he come Himself?"

"He did," Vivian said. "He became you and came here as you. If you don't know this, then you are 'dead' not in some other life but in this one."

DREAMS DEFINE

OUR SPIRITUAL DESTINY

The Swiss psychologist, Carl G. Jung, was said to have analyzed more than 60,000 dreams in his lifetime and he wrote a great deal about them. He did not consider them trivial or unworthy of serious study, obviously, or he would not have invested such an enormous amount of time and energy in this pursuit.

"Some dreams neither doctor nor patient understands," he said, but he regarded all dreams as meaningful just the same. "Or," he declared, "I wouldn't have the courage to deal with them."

"Dreams to me are links in a chain of inward invisible growth, reflecting whether we are developing spiritually, or whether that growth is static," said Vivian Heeschen, the California woman whose work with San Francisco Bay area people provided the basis for these discussions.

"I have not begun to probe a fraction of the number of dreams that Carl Jung did, but dreams are crystal clear for me in this respect. Our dreams either mark our progress, or demonstrate that we are merely 'marking time.'"

She insisted that we should attempt to interpret our daily lives as we would a dream, along specific guidelines. Here they are as I understand them: [1] Regard yourself not as one among many millions of dreamers but as The Dreaming One, for all dreams are God's dreams of Himself; [2] Understand yourself as having spiritual identity, not as just an organism with physical, mental, and emotional identity, that has departed from a pristine sense of Self for educative purposes in this three-dimensional world; [3] Consider that your consciousness is your spiritual reality and all else is tempor-reality, and that seven basic aspects of Consciousness are responsible for all of what we see as manifestation. These are: Mind, Principle, Spirit, Soul, Life, Truth, and Love, expressing themselves concretely, yielding evidence to ourselves and others as to just how deeply we sleep to Self-awareness, or how awake we are; [4] Life's purpose is to wake to this higher sense of Self, to move through it progressively, and transcend it consciously. We are established actively on such a track when we interpret the events of our daily life as we do the events of our dreams as different expressions of the same activity: God understanding Himself through the interactions of the characters peopling our dream world and our daily waking world; [5] Having embarked on this course deliberately and sincerely, the intuitive faculty within you begins to enliven and to aid you in this understanding. The character of your dream life changes to confirm your sincerity and your daily drama acquires meaning that it did not have for you before, equally as corroborative of your development as the night dream.

"Will you interpret an interesting dream for me?" I asked Vivian.

"Surely, what is it?"

"In this dream," I said, "two men met on a sidewalk outside a restaurant, an older man and a younger man. The older man was striking in that he had blue hair. From his pocket he took a round, flat piece of shiny machined metal and handed it to the younger man saying, 'Can you take this apart?' The young man looked at what had been given to him. It was a ring within a ring that moved seemingly on an axle that allowed the inner ring to turn at right angles to the outer ring. The inner edge of the outer had a notch in one place. The outer edge of the inner ring had a corresponding mark. When the two were aligned the young man pressed on the inner ring and the two snapped apart. 'This is a form of universal joint,' the old man explained. 'It is useful in the efficient operation of engines in the arctic at temperatures of 68 degrees below zero, and in the hottest deserts where it runs at 240 degrees.' With that, the old man took the piece back from the young man and walked away."

"To me," Vivian said, "the old man represents Spiritual Identity. His hair is blue. He is the spirit of Truth itself. The two circles of machined metal mean a universal joining into wholeness. They symbolize that. I'm not a numerologist but when numbers appear in dreams I reduce them to see which of the aspects of Consciousness they relate to. The number '68' adds to '14,' which adds to '5,' the fifth day of creation, or Life. The number '240' adds to '6' and can't be reduced further. The number 'six' stands for the sixth day of creation, or Truth. When the old man says to the young man as he hands him the symbol of wholeness, 'Can you take this apart?' it means, 'can you separate the truth from life?' It's a way of saying, 'Can you discern spiritual meaning--true meaning--in the mundane?' With that he walks away. This is a challenge to the one who is not yet conscious of his divinity to pursue that course. He has been handed that faculty that governs all extremes, all opposites, and he has been asked, 'Can you take this apart?' And he does! The faculty of intuitive insight, of discernment, is present with him. All he needs do is exercise it and augment his spiritual awakening. Wow! What a dream!" Vivian exclaimed.

"Would you believe it wasn't a dream?" I rejoined. "This actually happened to me one day as I was going into a restaurant. I'll never forget this incident with the blue-haired man. Why his hair had been tinted so, I don't know, but it was striking. He was leaving the restaurant, waiting for his wife to catch up with him as she was talking to someone behind him, and that was our conversation as I've told it to you."

Vivian laughed. "Do you see what I mean when I say that life is like unto a dream? We don't know how often we are called upon to enact roles like this in our daily lives, for the purpose of communicating meaning that is not always obvious, except where the intuitive faculty is active and able to translate the mundane.

"Whether that incident happened to you in front of a restaurant in our everyday waking world, or while lying fast asleep on your bed at night, it became a memory recording, a mental image. If it was another's experience instead of yours, and he told it to you, would it have less reality for you for having been his dream? The theater in which any scene is enacted is secondary to the enactment, if the meaning is understood. What we commonly call reality is only a classified reference to where an event took place."

Dreams are living Scripture: this was one of Vivian's favorite themes. "The *Bible* tells us there are two states," she said, "the 'quick' and the 'dead.' We can't be both since we must be one or the other. So we are either convinced of our divinity through experience, or we aren't.

"How much more do you want from dreams than that?" she asked when people questioned her as to whether dreams predict our future. "What kind of future do you think you'll have if you fail to lay claim to your most precious birthright?"

As she ended what she had to say to me, I could only reflect that the *Bible* says that Esau sold what was rightfully his for a mess of pottage.

- END -

AFTERTHOUGHTS:

PARTICULARLY FOR THE YOUNG

Freedom Barry, an American who has devoted much of his life to advancing ideas on spiritual wakening, once said, "You, as Consciousness, are not contained by the dream. You contain it. It only seems as though you are contained by it while the dream is on."

Can anything in a dream awaken The Dreamer?

"No," Mr. Barry replied to that question, "The Dreamer awakens spontaneously."

The characters in your night dream do not know they are being dreamt. They do not know they are products of The Dreamer's mentation and have no life of their own apart from The One who voluntarily entered the dream to enliven it.

The surrender of Consciousness (God) to the life of the dream is so total, so complete, that characters cannot be convinced they are animated concepts. "All that is present," Barry said again and again, "is Consciousness interpreting and understanding Itself in Its language of persons in places doing things."

I met a man who told me a remarkable dream that illustrates this.

He said he was a U.S. Marine in World War II. He had been wounded in the leg on Okinawa. After the war, he was flown to a hospital in Japan.

"While recovering from my wound," he told me, "I had a strange dream. I found myself in a beautiful ballroom resembling a medieval European palace. The ladies and men were dressed in white and wore powdered wigs. The ladies wore hoop skirts. The men wore knee breeches and had silver buckles on their shoes. We were dancing to soft, stately music and I said to the lady in my arms, 'All this is a dream! I'm a wounded soldier lying on a hospital bed and all of you are dream figures.' She stiffened and reacted, 'Oh, you've had a little too much to drink from the punch bowl!' 'No! It's true!' I retorted. 'Then maybe you'd better have one more to straighten you out!' she rebuked as she led me off the dance floor to the punch bowl. 'It's all a dream!' I protested, so loudly that everyone stopped dancing and came over to see what was the matter. 'This man is out of his mind!' my partner burst out. 'He says we are all a part of a dream he is having!' I got worked up. 'Yes!' I exclaimed. I then raised so much fuss that several men closed in. They were overpowering me. But as they were about to pin me down--poof! like a puff of smoke it all vanished. I found myself back on my hospital bed!"

I marvelled then, and still do.

He looked at me intently. His voice was heavy with emotion. He said with more than necessary emphasis, "Do you know what? When you die, nothing happens! All that happens is that you wake up!" Then he added, "WE ARE ALL GOING TO WAKE UP!"

Right-o. If you don't wake to see this life play as a dream on a different density than the night dream, you are no more than a dreamt character-- dead to the realization of being THE DREAMER.

Although John Baptist is made to say of Jesus, "He must increase, but I must decrease," meaning that the personal sense of self must give way to the divine sense of Self in spiritual awakening, persona resists awakening.

In the 1980's, a popular television show host often said in bemusement to his viewers, "I get these wild, crazy dreams and I just don't know what they mean! Last night I dreamt I was on board an airliner at Kennedy International Airport, taking off for Los Angeles. As we rose into the air, I shouted, 'Stop! I don't want to go! Let me off at 50th and Second!'"

Then as though he could hardly believe what he was about to say to his audience he said, "And, you know? That great big airplane swooped down into Manhattan without touching any of the buildings and let me off at the corner of 50th Street and Second Avenue! Then it turned and went on its way to Los Angeles without me. Now, what does that mean?" and he went on with his show.

Literal dream interpreters might say it means he has a chance for a better job in Los Angeles, but that he doesn't want to leave New York City.

No. Gurdjieff would say it means that more of us have the possibility of awakening than do.

First, there must be a willing mind. Or to quote Scripture, "Many are called but few are chosen," meaning it has to be a conscious choice on the part of the one invited to go to The City of Angels, the original name for Los Angeles in Spanish. He could reach a higher awareness but would rather remain in the sense-based sense of Self. The "50th" and "Second" intersection in New York symbolizes the five senses and this world of duality.

He doesn't want awakening now. Big-time television has made him famous. Fame is his bag, today's young people would say. Fame is as much of a drug as LSD, marijuana, cocaine, or other so used chemicals.

The Drug Bag. The Fame Bag. The Money Bag. The Grab Bag. There are many kinds of bags.

What is a brown paper bag?

Well, you know what a dark brown taste is. A brown paper bag comes out of the mouth and canopies the head like a helmet of thick, opaque bubblegum.

Oscar Wilde described us: "Most people are other people. Their thoughts are someone else's opinions, their lives a mimicry, their passions a quotation."

It's hard to see the bags of conditioning all of us wear. It is easier to recognize those who are wearing such brown paper bags and don't know it.

They say such things as, "I have fabulous dreams at night but they aren't anything. I just regard them as extra entertainment and write them off as such."

They are some of our best and most sincere people.

"We hope that in time, if we persist, things will be as they ought to be," they say. They mean it. And they work at it.

But nothing gets better in time.

They don't see that the way things are is the way things were meant to be for the growth and expansion of Consciousness.

They don't want to wake up and come out of their bag. They prefer to stay in it and try to have it more rosy and comfortable.

You can't have it both ways.

Destiny is to wake out of Life. Not to find a better dream in which to slumber.

Of course, if you're in prison it's better to have prison privileges than not to have them. But who wants to be imprisoned? Don't take this wrongly. There is nothing the matter with trying to improve this life's conditions. I'm not donning a hair shirt against those who pursue material well-being.

It's a part of the game Consciousness is playing as the players. However, there are different kinds of hair shirts, just as there are different bags. Striving to be more comfortable in a dream can be one of the most discomforting occupations.

This is not an argument for complacency in the face of all that needs doing in the world. If you think things can't get any worse, you're either unaware of what is going on, or you are already as bad off as you can get. It is easy--too easy--to retreat into quiet complacency and call it repose rather than resignation.

The mystic enjoys both resignation and repose in a way that others do not understand. The mystic dwells in a world of all-encompassing One-ness. Experiencing such a state alters one's perspective forever. You cannot be the same as before when you return to your "waking" reality of being one among many. You know it is only temporarily real while Consciousness is focused where you have physical form. The truth of being is that in Consciousness there is no separation from all others. There is only one Consciousness. Not two, not four, not 50, or 50 billion. One, only one.

The mystic does not shirk from doing his share while still here. He follows the dictum of Dr. Maurice Nicoll in his excellent volumes on psycho-transformation and is a "good householder" in life. He is equal to life. He doesn't look for a "cop out," because to cop out is to cop out against Oneself. That he can never do.

Some of the bags people wear are browner than others. Such as those who say dreams are nothing more than the psychic rehash of the corned beef you ate last night.

Or those who believe that dreams are disguised sex hang-ups.

They are into a bag of the rawest sienna.

Everybody is, has been, or will be repressed in some way, sexually or otherwise, before the Earth trip is over.

It's par for the course.

"Everything comes alike to all," Ecclesiastes tells us. One portion of repression per customer, along with its opposite, is handed out when you come sliding down the birth canal.

There are lots of ways to wear one's brown paper bag: with dignity, with pride, with arrogance. Some even stick feathers on them and wear them to the Easter Parade.

But one of the worst ways to wear your bag, kids, is with your head down, like you're looking for something and expecting to find it there.

Take those who fritter away time trying to stuff ESP messages into the heads of sleepers. Sure, images can be transferred, but only apparently so. In One Mind there isn't anywhere for them to go. Regardless of what cards turn up where, The Dealer still holds the deck.

And, asleep or awake, every play is His play.

How do you get on good terms with The Dreamer in you? Recognize IT, or "Jesus," if you're Christian, as the You that you really are, rather than the you you've always thought yourself to be--if that isn't too heavy.

There are some who think they have their heads out of the bag when they are merely wearing it like a choke collar. The Scriptures say, "Awake!" They don't tell you to swallow acid or drugs and go to sleep thinking you've reached enlightenment.

There are many persons in that bag, especially young ones. Hopefully, you're not one who is giving himself or herself an ersatz nirvana to see if cocaine or vicious addictive trippers will bring it to you.

You've got a head contraction, if you call that expansion.

And anyone who promotes the philosophy of "turning in, turning on, and dropping out" with drugs deserves a smack in the nose.

You aren't any different, any better, or any worse than anyone else in the awakening from this life dream, this drama of "good-and-evil." Sooner than some, later than others, but no better or worse.

This gets your head out of the bag a little way, now doesn't it?

Why not come all the way out? You'll like it. You may have scary dreams on the way out, without drugs. Some of them will be filled with such wonder and beauty and joy and laughter that they will remain with you as long as you draw breath. If you don't understand that all dreams, no matter their quality, are an accompaniment to your spiritual awakening from sleep, they'll continue to be scary. Or they may go away and leave you alone. That's about the worst thing that can happen to you, unless you're so "awake" in the dream of the day that nightly instruction is unnecessary.

Daily, you deal with things that are transient, that have no permanence. Your dreams are signals from Eternity. Only eternal things are real.

The highest conception of a dream is that it is a communication from Heaven to Earth, the earth of your inner world, which is like a seed-bed for growth when the soil is prepared. That preparation entails a radical turning of the mind as to who you are: The Dreamer, not one of the dreamt.

Artemidorus, an early Greek writer, wrote volumes on dreams. But about all that can be extracted from what he wrote is the idea that just about any interpretation of a dream is valid.

No, not if you wish to become nutrient soil for transforming ideas that reach Man from a source beyond this physical world.

God, being the Author of Dreams, and God, being the rewarder of them that diligently seek Him, you have the right to expect results in being able to remember and understand your dreams.

Pray to have your dream life enlivened. But don't pray unless you can stand a good deal of chastisement, embarrassment, and pain. To become whole requires stripping away all that is false and useless. There is much of this in us that cannot be seen until the surface mind is closed down in nightly slumber.

It takes time to flush out the Augean Stables.

To condense, you're stuck with this world and you can't get unstuck from it because, as person, you're not doing it.

When Consciousness wants to get unstuck, to relieve Itself from having lived, as you, It will do it. And take you with It, with no loss of your identity and uniqueness.

And that's the only hope you have.

We are all brown bagging it together. When the time comes for you to be removed from the bag you're in, it is said, ". . . of that day and that hour knoweth no man."

So, "watch," Scripture says. Stay alert. Interpret your daily life as you do a dream. See it as a monologue staged in dialogues. Consciously live life from moment to moment. Don't permit yourself to be lived unconsciously by Life.

This may not be the time for the bag--the mask, to come off. Yet "now" is the only time it ever will. So if this isn't the hour, no matter. All this book will do is help you get ready for destiny when It announces Itself. So you'll know what's happening.

And that's quite a bit.

Until then, "keep on keeping on." Play out the end of your string, whatever it's tied to.

But don't get spaced out doing it.

In the interim, keep in mind these few words of wisdom from the *I Ching*: "The Wild Goose gradually draws near the tree. Perhaps it will find a flat branch. No blame."

When it comes time to take off the bag, do so.

Pop it!

And make a joyful noise unto the Lord.

TO DREAM OF KNOWING

IS TO KNOW OF DREAMING

Pull the lever of sleep over the eyes of humanity, nightly, and it's the dream jackpot.

All the imaged characters of every Ray Bradbury story, and more, are on stage all at once.

From the gaping side of the Illustrated Man, Las Vegas comes tumbling out of the slot. Dazzling strip of neon casinos. Glittering rhinestoned setting for sleek black limousines and tall ermine-wrapped showgirls, high-stepping, Eve-like, from Adam's Rib.

Then in kaleidoscopic fashion the image splits into an arachnoid membrane. With every indrawn breath The Dreamer takes on His primeval bed, living mandalas form and shatter. Deep now in dark Costeauian seas of squid shapes, black inks of octopi issuing red through arterial and venous networks, delicate coral brains throb in skull jackets of human generation, enlivened by the primordial urge to know some other than Itself, and by such knowing, Self, Itself, define.

From dark seas dark forests gloom, swamps slime. Waterfalls cascade and orchid blooms burst from cauldrons of volcanic suns, the scalding

landscape steamy with Leviathan roars as great rep-
tilian shapes locked in combat echo the quakes of
creation.

Ages of ice and snow entomb in crystal the
once living flesh. Then melting and reforming, the
kaleidoscope picks up shards and fragments of mentation from the periphery of infinity, spearing them
into target center where straight lines and angles
turn into whorls and spirals, out to the circumference
of moats, moonlight bathed, the deep well of in-
choate beginnings from which swim squirming tad-
poles borne on raven wings of Poe-like blackness,
rushing with a billion watery, windmill sounds up,
up, to the light to crawl and dry and rise and walk
and climb and fly and soar and create in the image
of the unseen Imager, his proud civilizations, now
burial mounds and launching pads for new thrusts as
he hurls his cities skyward and flings himself after
them.

Talcum tracings on the windows of the imagination. Frost flowers rinsing away in rainsweeps of
movement. The palette knife now busy yet again
spreading image after image over the inner canvas,
lightning storms against the black inner lids of sleep
condensing moisture drops of new fevers onto the
dream soaked screen of the still, immobilized mind.
Never taking the viewer behind the scenes to reveal
what Wizard stirs the crucible; only the effects witnessed, never The Causative Agent misted in the
alembics of cosmic alchemy. A montage of tinctures
and swirling smokes. Epic dreams of engagement
and disengagement, passions of love and hate,
whirling carousels of revelry and rage, a Mardi Gras

of madly turning chariot wheels, the lymph of Life twisting umbilically into view after displacing view, a Seurat-scape of pointillist light-and-shadow, a helix of hells and Harlequinades.

A Chinese emperor dreaming of a sleeping butterfly dreaming of a sleeping Chinese emperor dreaming. . . The Supine Man, tattooed from head to toe, rises, his illustrated skin sloughs off and turns into a huge dancing bear that he leads on a golden chain out into the light of beginningness all over again, standing sharp and clear in the mirror-well of imaginings that issue where The River of Sleep rises and runs toward a dawn that promises to burst but never does before The Dreamer stirs and finds that the night which He entered upon so long ago is nothing but a stretch of moments immeasurable except by the sundials and clock hands of experience.

You've been to bed and gotten up again and all the world's history cast into polarities of meeting and mating, of conflict and withdrawal, are dissolved in the matrix from which they issued. The vortex has vanished. You're awake now standing on the hard surface of your bedroom floor. Or are you still couch-bound in some invisible room you never remembered retiring to, dreaming what you call having wakened from a dream but dreaming still?

A butterfly passes by your open window and you breathe a sigh for you know now that you are not a butterfly dreaming that you are a man. But neither are you that which thinks it is a man seeing a butterfly.

You are That Which Conceives of dreaming and having so conceived, dreams, forgetting yourself to be The Conceiver whose conceptions know no life except the life with which you invest them; that the dream might be your only reality until some bell of your own setting reconstitutes The Dreamer whose potential now for redreaming is augmented to an exponential power beyond all calculation.

*   *   *

FINIS

All things are in motion,
Produced by mind's seeming;
A focus contracted,
The viewpoint of dreaming.

But until he knows
The ultimate cause,
Man dwells in a maze
Of multiple laws.

By taking the truth
Of a sensory thing,
He measures the world
With the length of a string.

And when he awakes
To discover his plan,
God knows that he slept
In his image, as Man.

- Vivian Heeschen

ADDENDUM

The following resources and references are excellent for anyone who is interested in probing the meaning of dream-time messages that issue to all of us during nightly sleep:

Harold Bayley, *The Lost Language of Symbolism* [Originally published in 1912 in London; now published in the U.S.A. by Rowman & Littlefield, New Jersey 07512].

J. E. Cirlot, *A Dictionary of Symbols* [Philosophical Library, New York City].

G. A. Gaskell, *Dictionary of All Scriptures and Myths* [Avenel Books, distributed by Crown Publishers, Inc., New York City].

Metaphysical Bible Dictionary [Unity School of Christianity, Unity Village, MO 64065].

Jack Ensign Addington, *The Hidden Mystery of The Bible* [Perigee Books, 200 Madison Avenue, New York City, 10016].

Additionally, those who wish to pursue the meaning and purpose of sentient life are commended to the writings and the tape recorded lectures of the late Neville Goddard, a 20th-century Christian mystic, whose many books are published posthumously by DeVorss & Company, P. O. Box 550, Marina del Rey, CA 90291. DeVorss distributes to book stores nationally.

A treasure trove of Neville's Los Angeles lectures preserved on audio cassette tapes may be obtained by writing to Canterbury House, 8726 South Sepulveda Blvd., Suite 18, Los Angeles, CA 90045. A list of Neville's San Francisco lectures on cassette may be obtained by writing J & L Publications, P. O. Box 360, Trinity Center, CA 96091.

For those readers who are not acquainted with Neville, his books and his teaching, a biographical sketch of this original thinker follows.

Gopi Krishna makes this statement: "Humankind is slowly evolving towards a sublime state of consciousness of which fleeting glimpses have been afforded to us by the great seers and mystics of past and present."[1]

From Sri Arobindo we get this: "What is behind appearance in this seeming mystery? Consciousness losing Itself, returning to Itself, emerging from Self-forgetfulness. . . to be again divinely Self-conscious, free, infinite, immortal."[2]

To this Neville would add: "Only through contraction can God expand His creative power. He is what we are, we are what He is in this process."

---

[1] Gopi Krishna, *The Biological Basis of Religion and Genius*, [New York City, 1972].

[2] Sri Arobindo, *The Life Divine*, [Arya, August 1914–January 1919. S.A., Ashram Press, Pondicherry, India].

NEVILLE GODDARD

1905 - 1972

Joseph Murphy, a writer and lecturer, who studied with Neville in New York City, said of him: "Neville eventually may be recognized as one of the world's great mystics."

Born on the island of Barbados in the British West Indies, Neville was the fourth child in a family of nine boys and one girl.

One day some of them were playing near an old wind-swept hut by the sea. A seer lived in the hut and told them their fortunes. The elder sons would go into the professions, into medicine, into business. These predictions came true. Today, the Goddard family is one of the most prominent and influential families in Barbados and the surrounding islands.

"Do not touch the fourth one," the seer said, pointing to Neville, "he has a special mission to perform in the world—from God." And to Neville, "You will journey to a distant land and spend your life there."

This prediction also came true. As a young man he went to America and worked for J. C. Penney and Macy's. Later, he worked in the theater with the Schuberts.

Under unusual circumstances, he met a black Jew, named Abdullah, who lectured on Christianity. Neville went to hear him, somewhat under protest, to satisfy the constant urging of a friend, "Whose judgment I did not respect," Neville said, "because he made such poor financial investments."

Neville said, "I was seated in the auditorium waiting for the lecture to begin, when the speaker--who I had never seen before--came down the aisle from the rear of the auditorium to the stage."

"You are late, Neville!" Abdullah admonished, "six months' late! I have been told to expect you." From this introduction, Neville studied with Abdullah seven days a week for seven years.

"Abdullah taught me Hebrew, he taught me The Kabbalah, and he taught me more about real Christianity than anyone I ever met," Neville later declared.

Neville travelled throughout the U.S., appearing on the stage and on television, finally settling in Los Angeles which he made his base of operation. In the 1960's and early '70s, he confined most of his lectures to Los Angeles, San Francisco, and New York.

Neville contended that our Judeo-Christian *Bible*'s importance is not in its historicity, but in its vision of The Journey of the Soul: a document blueprinting the experience of Everyman, culminating in the discovery by each of us that we are The Christ. He was adamant in his insistence that The Book "--is not secular history. Each of us is destined to discover that he is The Father, God Himself, and the *Bible*--as originally written--was a collection of the testimonials of those who, in ancient times made this discovery. These unknown New Testament authors wrote their accounts in the third person, not in the first, knowing the reader eventually would come to realize that from cover to cover, The Book is all about himself."

This discovery Neville called God's "Promise." There is nothing any person can do to earn it. It is sheer Grace and comes to you in its own good time.

If you do not experience it before you die, then what?

"You pass through a door--that's all that death is," Neville said, "and you are restored to life instantly in a world like this--just this world," he was fond of saying with a sweep of his hand, "and you go on there with the same problems you had here with no loss of identity--not old, not blind, not crippled, if you depart this life that way, but young. They grow and they marry, and they die there, too, with all the fear of death that we have here. If they die there without experiencing The Promise, they are restored to life again and again in a place best suited to the work yet to be done on them. It continues until 'Christ be formed in you' and as 'sons of The Resurrection' you leave this world of death never to enter it again."

"You are born only <u>once</u> through the womb of woman, <u>once</u> from above," Neville insisted, "you don't go through any womb again."

What about the fear many have of hell and damnation? In response to this often asked question, Neville replied with a quote from Scripture, "'Not one shall be lost in all my holy mountain.' You and God are One, and how could God eternally condemn Himself?"

Until we awaken individually and make this discovery, we are privileged to use a Law, given by

God, to "cushion the blows of life." The Law, stated succinctly, is this in Neville's own words: "Imagining creates reality."

In his lectures and books, Neville dealt solely with The Law until the year 1959, "For I did not know of The Promise until that summer and continuing during the next three-and-one-half years. This is Scriptural," he would say, "read it in the Book of Daniel where it is referred to as 'a time, times, and a half.' A year in the ancient calendar was 360 days long. A 'time' then, plus twice a 'time' and half a 'time,' comes to 1260 days in your experience of it. It is referred to yet again, more enigmatically in the Book of Revelation."

In his use of The Law, Neville related how he made a sea voyage from New York to see his family in Barbados during the Depression years, without any money of his own. He also related how by the use of imaginal power he was honorably discharged from military service to continue his lectures during World War II. In San Francisco in the '50s and '60s, he gave his audiences accounts of how others had made use of The Law. He discussed it on television in Los Angeles. "Learn how to use your imaginal power, lovingly, for Man is moving into a world where everything is subject to his imaginal power," Neville taught.

In the latter part of the 1960's and early '70s, Neville emphasized The Promise after he had experienced it. The use of imaginal power can change circumstances but it is all temporary, "--and will vanish like smoke," he asserted with another sweep of his hand. "Oh, you can use it to make a fortune, to become known in the world--all these things are done--but your true purpose here is to fulfill Scripture." So he subordinated The Law to The Promise and became as eager to hear accounts from those who had experienced The Promise as he had of those with The Law.

In his last years Neville said, "I know my time is short. I have finished the work I have been sent here to do. I am now eager to depart. I know I will not appear in this three-dimensional world again for The Promise has been fulfilled in me. As for where I go? I will know you there as I have known you here --for we are all brothers, infinitely in love with each other."

Neville spoke without notes and he followed his lectures with questions from the audience. When asked if he had tapes of his lectures for sale he responded, "I have no tapes. Others here are making tapes for their own use. Perfectly all right, but I have no tapes."

Thanks to the loyalty of his students, Neville's voice and thought have been preserved for posterity. He left our Earth plane on October 1, 1972.

*   *   *

FREEDOM BARRY

This book cannot be ended without a few words about author-lecturer Freedom Barry, a Biblical scholar and teacher of individual spiritual awakening. He is the only instructor in this field who had Neville's enthusiastic endorsement. In 1963, he wrote and self-published *I Do*, an exhortative little book which continues to be a cherished treasure to many of its owners. Now in retirement years, Freedom Barry's available writing time has increased. 1992 saw the publication of *Passkey* and yet more books are planned for the future. *I Do* and *Passkey* are available in book stores nationally or by writing J & L Publications.

*   *   *

Author **Vern Hansen** has had careers as a metallurgical analyst, broadcasting promotion specialist, Air Force Special Services officer, and an industrial advertising manager. Presently a free-lance writer, he has written human interest articles for numerous publications. He lives in Los Gatos, California.

*   *   *